ROUTLEDGE LIBRARY EDITIONS: HISTORY OF THE MIDDLE EAST

Volume 6

THE GULF STATES AND OMAN

THE GULF STATES AND OMAN

CHRISTINE OSBORNE

Routledge
Taylor & Francis Group
LONDON AND NEW YORK

First published in 1977 by Croom Helm Ltd

This edition first published in 2017
by Routledge
2 Park Square, Milton Park, Abingdon, Oxon OX14 4RN

and by Routledge
711 Third Avenue, New York, NY 10017

Routledge is an imprint of the Taylor & Francis Group, an informa business

© 1977 Christine Osborne

All rights reserved. No part of this book may be reprinted or reproduced or utilised in any form or by any electronic, mechanical, or other means, now known or hereafter invented, including photocopying and recording, or in any information storage or retrieval system, without permission in writing from the publishers.

Trademark notice: Product or corporate names may be trademarks or registered trademarks, and are used only for identification and explanation without intent to infringe.

British Library Cataloguing in Publication Data
A catalogue record for this book is available from the British Library

ISBN: 978-1-138-22002-7 (Set)
ISBN: 978-1-315-39118-2 (Set) (ebk)
ISBN: 978-1-138-22004-1 (Volume 6) (hbk)
ISBN: 978-1-138-22030-0 (Volume 6) (pbk)
ISBN: 978-1-315-41329-7 (Volume 6) (ebk)

Publisher's Note
The publisher has gone to great lengths to ensure the quality of this reprint but points out that some imperfections in the original copies may be apparent.

Disclaimer
The publisher has made every effort to trace copyright holders and would welcome correspondence from those they have been unable to trace.

The Gulf States and Oman

The Gulf States and Oman

Text and Photographs
Christine Osborne

CROOM HELM LONDON

Abu Dhabi, the boom city.

© 1977 Christine Osborne
Croom Helm Ltd, 2-10 St John's Road, London SW11

ISBN 0-85664-515-X

British Library Cataloguing in Publication Data

Osborne, Christine
   The Gulf States and Oman.
   1. Petroleum industry and trade – Arabian
   Peninsula – Gulf States   2. Arabian Peninsula –
   Social conditions
   I. Title
   309.1'53'605   HN766

ISBN 0-85664-515-X

My Mother

Printed in Great Britain
by Redwood Burn Ltd, Trowbridge and Esher

Contents

Prologue	6
Maps	8
Introduction	14
1. Bahrain	17
2. Kuwait	34
3. Qatar	48
4. The United Arab Emirates	61
Abu Dhabi	63
Dubai	88
Sharjah	105
Ajman	115
Umm al Qaiwain	117
Ras al-Khaimah	120
Fujairah	127
5. The Sultanate of Oman	130
6. The Vanishing Bedouin	156
The Camel	166
Falconry	171
Costume and Accoutrements	178
7. The Emerging Women of the Gulf	185
Appendix	201
Bibliography	205
Index	207

Prologue

When the increase in oil prices resulted in the energy crisis of 1974-5, the West reacted with bitter attacks against the Arabs and the media created its stereotype, a blend of Bedouin, guerrilla and playboy.

Few races suffer as much from typecasting as the Arabs, particularly the peoples of the excessively wealthy Gulf States: Kuwait, Qatar, the United Arab Emirates, Bahrain and the Sultanate of Oman.

Largely ignorant of the Gulf, I decided to visit Dubai, one of the Arab Emirates, on my way to Australia in 1974. The week I left, a British Airways plane was hijacked from Dubai to Tunis and the Gulf Arabs were the subject of further spurious stories. For my part, I found Dubai to be so interesting that I stopped in the Gulf again, on my return to London.

This time, I also visited Abu Dhabi, Bahrain and Kuwait, by now enthralled, for everywhere great cities were mushrooming in the desert and a whole culture was having to adjust to unprecedented social change.

Oil, their *raison d'être,* is buying the Gulf Arabs what some people call 'civilisation', what others label as 'Westernisation', and what is best described as comforts, in one of the harshest climates on earth.

The social effects of this swift transition from pearling and trading economies to some of the wealthiest countries in the world are enormous. In the process, the Bedouin, who once comprised 40 per cent of the population, are a vanishing race.

Although it was a decided disadvantage to be a Western woman journalist in the Gulf, the real hurdle lay in writing a book on a contemporary subject, such as the Gulf State oil producers. However, the book is finished, and the frustrations known to all familiar with the Gulf are almost forgotten — certainly the desert and its peoples taught me something of life that I would have missed, had I not decided to visit Dubai.

There are many people to thank, foremost Mr Douglas Ditton of British Airways. Also Gulf Air and Singapore Airlines.

In Bahrain, Australian Trade Commissioner Mr Phillip King, Mr Anwar Mohamed, Mr David Nicoll and the Ministry of Information.

The Kuwait Hilton, Mr Faysal Suhaib and Lieutenant-Colonel Bader al-Sayegh.

The Ministry of Information in Qatar. Mr Hassan al-Samra, Mr Ibrahim al-Obaid and Mr Abdullah al-Nowas, of the Ministry of Information in Abu Dhabi.

A special thanks to Michael Daly, the Abu Dhabi Hilton, Mr Mohamed H. Nujumi and Dr. Morsy Abdullah.

To my numerous drivers in Abu Dhabi.

To Mr Patrick Board, General Manager of the Dubai Inter-Continental Hotel and Mrs Yvonne Chetwin curator of the Dubai Museum. Also Mr Elias Bahou, of Dubai Real Estate.

Mr Bart Paff, Economic Adviser to His Highness Sheikh Sultan, ruler of Sharjah.

In the Sultanate of Oman, Mr Abdul Aziz M. Rowas, Under-Secretary of the Ministry of Information.

Lieutenant-Colonel J. Trelawny, Commanding Officer of Sultan's Armed Forces.

Mr Morrison Johnston of Michael Rice Associates in London, Mr Colin Fitch of Anthony Gibb, London and particularly Ms Aileen Aitken, Cabin Crew Superintendant, who test flew British Airways' Concorde.

And to the expatriates and Arabs who helped me on that long, hot trek through the Gulf and to the many friends who encouraged me, in England and Australia – *shokran!*

Christine Osborne

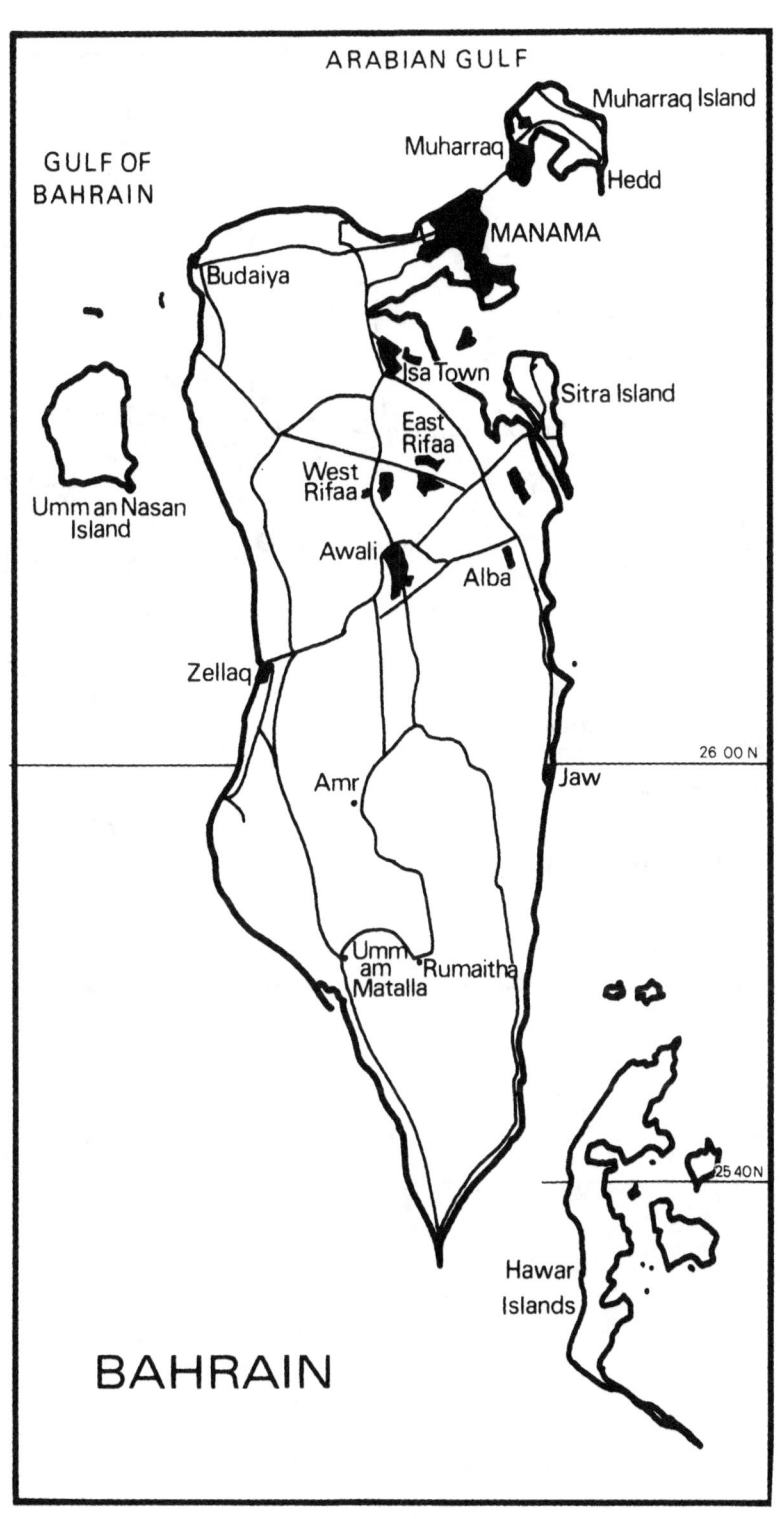

KUWAIT

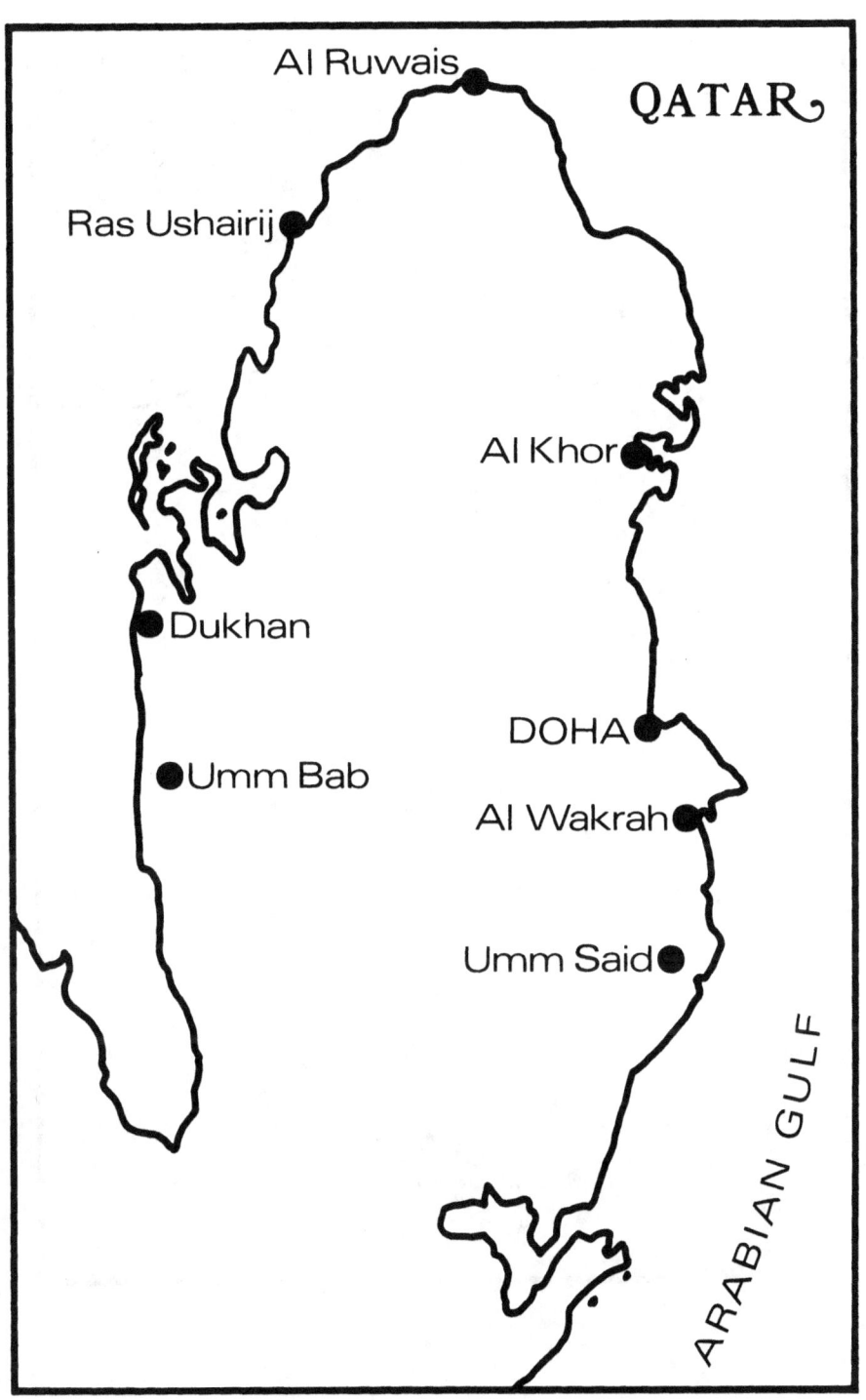

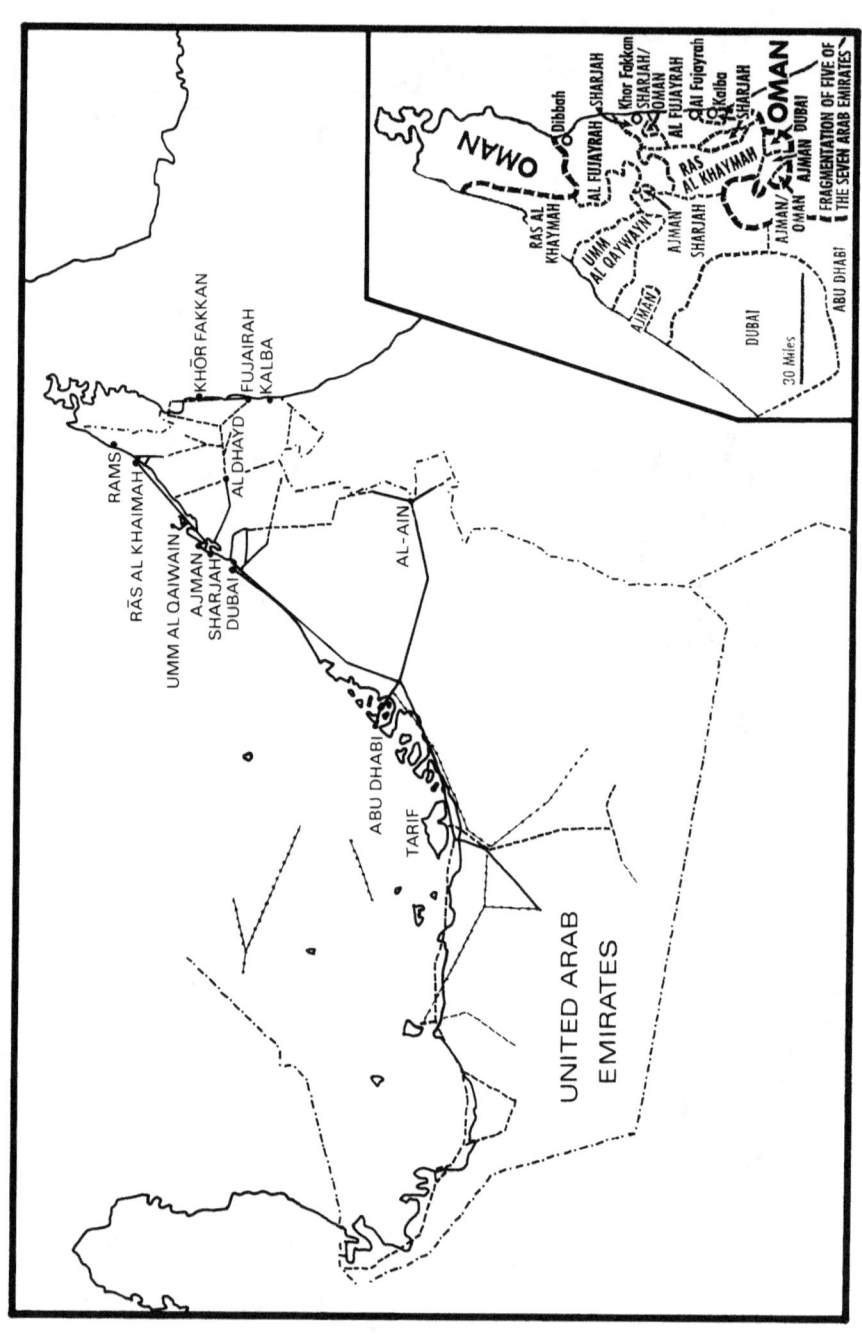

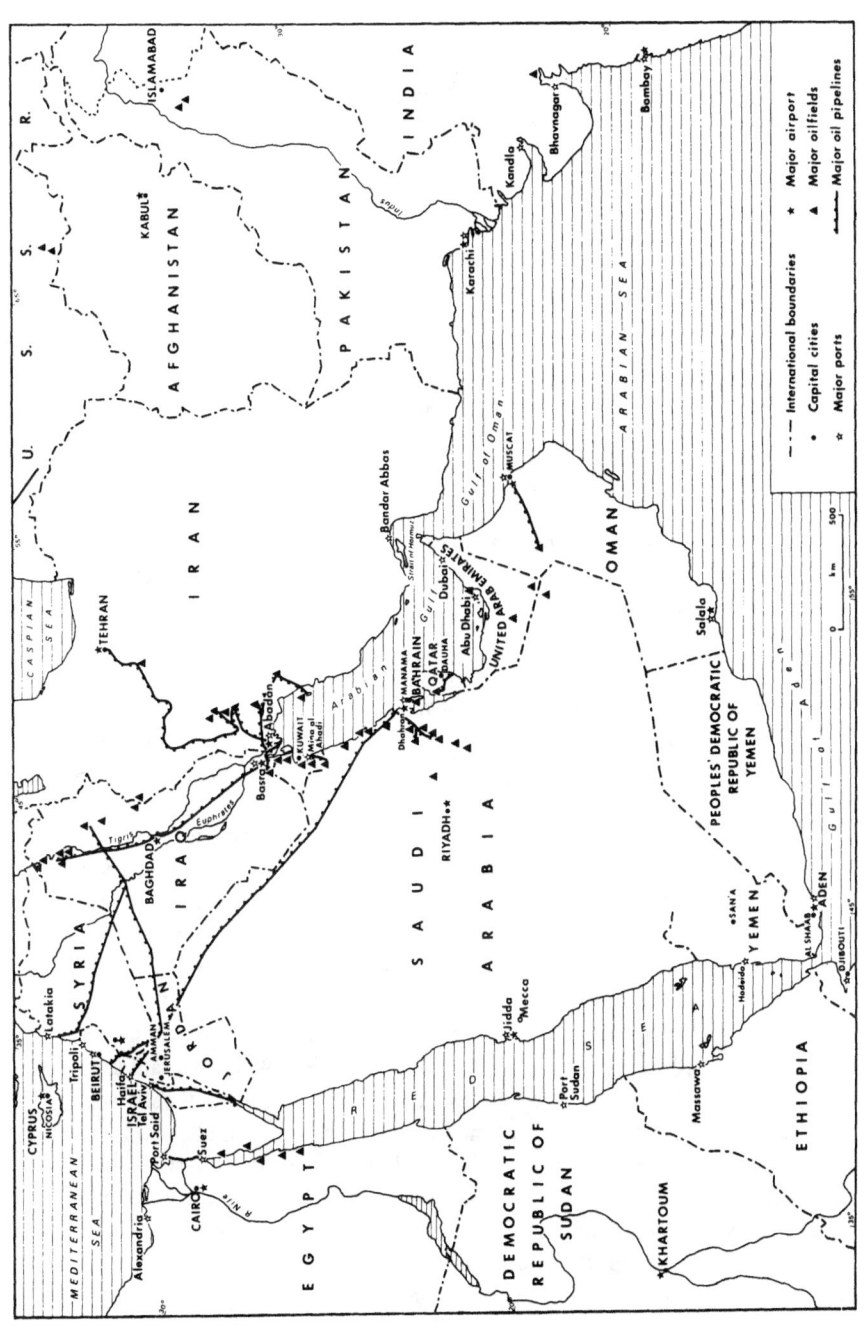

Introduction

When making a comparison between the Gulf States, the most important thing to remember is the date when oil came on-stream.

Obviously those Emirates, or sheikhdoms, which first discovered oil are more advanced in terms of what I shall call *Westernisation* — Bahrain and Kuwait, for instance, as opposed to the United Arab Emirates and Oman. The Sultanate of Oman is something of an exception since the country only revived when Sultan Qaboos assumed power in 1970, but in the interim, many Omanis were able to educate themselves abroad.

But how does anyone behave on winning the pools?

He buys a new house, a car, invests, takes a holiday, in fact he behaves in exactly the same way as the new Gulf oil millionaires, except that they are more generous. In 1970, Abu Dhabi gave so much money away that it almost went bankrupt.

Certainly some of the desert courtesies have been replaced by greed, but the Gulf Arab remains the most hospitable of men and the West would do well to adopt some traditions from Bedouin civilisation.

There are many tales one could tell in a book such as this, like the UAE Minister who owns a hundred cars, or the Kuwaiti sheikh who, after a night's romp with a Lebanese singer, asked which colour, of the four Cadillacs parked outside, did she prefer? When she said she could not decide, he told her to take them all. All this is relative, as before the discovery of oil, they would have been camels.

One unfortunate aspect of the sudden acquisition of vast wealth is the duplication of so many projects in order to have the best and impress the West, in the Gulf Arabs' search for status. If tribal conflicts ended in 1899 with the 'Treaty of Peace in Perpetuity', economic battles are now being waged in the doubling up of docks, airports and aluminium smelters, all along the Gulf.

Then there is the prestige competition, or what can be called 'the great Gulf monuments race'. Who can build the tallest building, the fastest flyover, the splashiest fountain, the biggest conference centre, the largest roundabout and ultimately, the most expensive earth station?

A Minister summed it up when he said that unless the Gulf States find a common plan to co-ordinate development, they will soon be fighting each other for industrial markets.

'How can I, as a Gulf citizen, comprehend the duplication of economic projects?' he said. 'The building of two huge dry docks and four earth stations? Where will it all end?'

And there is not only open competition between the sheikhdoms, but underlying hostilities between the rulers. Between Bahrain and Qatar over the Hawar Islands, between Abu Dhabi and Dubai for economic and political prestige, between Dubai and Sharjah over borders and likewise between Kuwait and Iraq.

Apart from obvious material changes brought by the oil boom, there have been marked changes in social values, especially among the Bedouin, for although there is still an enormous wealth gap between the classes, money and aid are definitely reaching the desert dwellers through generous welfare programmes.

'We *want* to adopt the good customs of the West', said Sheikha Fatima, wife of the Ruler of Abu Dhabi and founder of the 'Women's Movement' in Abu Dhabi.

Despite the new wealth affecting every aspect of the Gulf Arabs' lives, Islamic traditions are maintained. Whenever a Gulf Arab speaks, whether in business, or socially, he invariably introduces Islam into the conversation, not least in the oft-repeated *inshallah.*

Most of the older sheikhs are extremely religious and although the new generation does not go to the mosques, there is a parallel in young Christians not attending church. In any event, the Ministry of Islamic Affairs in the United Arab Emirates plans to build 445 new mosques by 1979.

The question is, what will happen to the Gulf States ten years from now? Some Western businessmen predict that everyone will have made his money and left. Others liken it, especially in the Emirates, to another Klondike. The rulers are aware their halcyon days are numbered and their behaviour in building as much as they can, as fast as they can, is normal from anyone given a multi-billion dollar blank cheque. Certainly the future of the Gulf States will be as interesting as their sudden début on the world stage.

Left alone with their oil revenues and advisers they will continue to develop, hopefully becoming self-sufficient in basic foodstuffs, wih world demand for oil and its by-products guaranteeing their economic growth.

But being so wealthy and so vulnerable, can they expect to remain unmolested? Historically, their Moslem neighbours have always asserted claims on the small Gulf States and the entire oil-rich Arabian peninsula risks assault from Communism.

The British presence provided a certain security in the past, but although Britain intervened in the 1955 Buraimi dispute with Saudi Arabia and protected Kuwait from Iraqi aggression, since its withdrawal from the Trucial States in 1971 and especially with North Sea oil on-stream, it is unlikely Britain would assist in any future confrontations.

Sultan Qaboos of Oman probably summed up the situation in his address marking the end of the guerrilla insurgency in Dhofar, in December 1975: 'Oman is the first Arab country to defeat international Communism on the battlefield. Therefore the Communists will not forget'.

1 Bahrain

The state of Bahrain is composed of a group of 35 islands with an area of approximately 255 square miles. It lies half-way down the Gulf, 15 miles east of Saudi Arabia and 17 miles north of Qatar. Most of the estimated population of 250,000 live on the largest island of Bahrain. Its capital is Manama which is connected by causeway to the adjacent island of Muharraq. The Emir of Bahrain is H.H. Sheikh Isa bin Sulman al-Khalifa, who declared his country independent on 15 August 1971, terminating all political and military ties with Britain.

Bahrain strikes a precise balance between East and West. In a supermarket or a night-club it seems like somewhere in Europe, but then the breeze carries a scent of spices and the sound of the *muezzin* calling people to the mosque.

The most striking sight in Bahrain is Concorde coming in to land above a dhow blowing across the bay. This contrast is only seen in Arabia, where life is in swift transition following the discovery of oil.

On 22 January 1976, Bahrain made aviation history as the first destination for supersonic travel. Concorde will ultimately fly the 11,500 miles between London and Melbourne, via Bahrain, in 14 hours, 15 minutes. Normal flights take up to 29 hours. The effect of leaving London on British Airways Concorde and arriving in the Gulf only four hours later is, as David Frost described it, 'like experiencing a taste of tomorrow today'.

Although Bahrain is today poor compared to its wealthy neighbours, it used to be the most prosperous place in the Gulf. Babylonian texts referred to it as 'Dilmun', the 'earthly paradise and rendezvous of gods'. In truth, because of its strategic location, plentiful fresh water and a flourishing pearl industry, the island was frequently besieged. Only in 1976 did the Shah drop Persia's historic claims on Bahrain.

The history of its present ruling family, the al-Khalifas, is closely

Concorde on her maiden flight to Bahrain.

« كونكورد » في أول رحلة لها إلى البحرين . يناير ١٩٧٥ .

tied to the al-Sabah sheikhs of Kuwait. Both are descended from the Bani Utbah tribe which lived in the Najd region of central Arabia until a particularly fierce summer in the eighteenth century forced them on to the coast. To benefit from the rich pearl beds off Bahrain, several of the al-Khalifa families moved south, from Kuwait to Zubara, on the west coast of Qatar. Welcomed by its inhabitants, they built a great fortress as their headquarters and commenced trading with Bahrain. Resenting the intrusion, the Mussallim rulers of Qatar attacked the fort, but were repelled.

As the al-Khalifa's prosperity grew, the Persians also bombarded the great fort, but from higher up the Gulf, the al-Sabahs moved south, blocking the Persian retreat via Bahrain, which was subsequently occupied by the al-Khalifas, together with many mainland Arabs. Shrewd businessmen, they soon built Bahrain into the most important entrepôt in the Gulf, but it was not until the nineteenth century that the island knew any form of peace. In order to safeguard it from further aggression, Ruler Sheikh Isa signed treaties with Britain. In return for British protection, Bahrain guaranteed not to sign any agreements with other foreign governments and it was not until independence that these ties were severed.

Bahrain has passed through three periods of great wealth: the

Copper Age, the Pearl Age and the Oil Age, but it was most prosperous during the Copper Age (from 3000 BC), when it was one of the most important trading centres in the ancient world. Most of the evidence is buried under the dunes, but a vast cemetery of more than 10,000 graves shows that its inhabitants must have been well-off, since only an affluent society could have afforded such elaborate, individual tombs in what is the largest tumulus cemetery in the world.

All Bahrain is rich in pre-historic remains. Excavations by Danish teams have discovered on the north coast what are supposedly the ruins of the capital of Dilmun. The site resembles little more than a rubbish heap of crumbling stones, weeds and soft-drink cans, but digging reveals relics of every civilisation that occupied Bahrain, as far back as the snakeworshippers of Dilmun.

The most important find was seven stamp seals. Similar seals, struck with the merchant's trade-mark, were discovered in Lower Mesopotamia, confirming the island's widespread trading contacts, and coins bearing the head of Alexander the Great were also found, indicating some trade with ancient Greece.

Pearling

The history of pearling delves deep into the past, to the days of Dilmun, when inscriptions referred to pearls as 'fishes' eyes', but it was in the nineteenth century that the industry reached a peak, when some 25,000 men were employed.

One of the most romantic sights of 'Old Gulf Coast' days was the start of the *Gaus al-Kabir,* the diving season, when hundreds of pearling boats set sail from Bahrain and, beating drums and singing sea shanties, the whole population lined Muharraq to bid farewell. As they worked, the crew also sang, led by a *naham*, chosen for his ability to lead in a high-pitched voice. Sometimes the tone was soft, like the *al-fijiri* or 'songs of dawn', when his voice rose slightly higher than the others, singing, almost mournfully, the sentimental pearling ballads. When the fleet arrived over the pearl banks, the divers donned dark trousers and bearing a basket round their backs, they stepped into loops of rope, weighed with coral lumps, and were lowered into the sea by a 'puller'. A clip of shell pinching their nose, they moved swiftly along the bottom, cutting the oysters off with a small, curved knife. After a minute's work, they signalled to be hauled up. A good diver could make 50-60 dives a day to 20 fathoms, eating and drinking only at dusk. The following morning, everyone squatted on the deck to open the shells, as pearls were found, either popping them in their mouths, or sticking them between their toes until handing them to the captain, or *nakhuda*.

The pearl merchants, or brokers acting on behalf of international firms, often did not wait for the fleet to return, but sailed out to bargain on the water. Only one buyer could go on board at a time so there was always a race when a big pearl was found. The whole pearling industry was well organised with commercial boats selling food and water, bank boats offering cash and loans, police boats patrolling for any skulduggery, even medical vessels making rounds.

Contrary to romantic belief, the divers were not troubled by sharks, saw-fish, or the giant clam-shell which made diving dangerous off Northern Australia. The worst trap in which a diver could find himself was literally with the *nakhuda*, the captain, and indeed many men sold themselves into a life of diving slavery. The captains frequently gave the divers far in excess of what was required to care for their families during their absence, so that because of debts they were forced to work for the same boat, season after season. Diving debts could also be bequeathed, so that if a father died owing money, a *nakhuda* could force his son to work until the amount was paid. Sheikh Isa's grandfather, Sheikh Sulman, abolished these malpractices, ruling that when a diver died, his debts were null and void, so that although the industry was reduced in size, men were able to dive if they wished, and not because they were obliged.

Bahrain pearls are reputed to have a special lustre which is said to result from the fresh-water springs bubbling in the surrounding sea. The best-known pearl is the 'Bahrain Pearl' which was sold to Barbara Hutton for £15,000, but there are many of greater value. I held one worth £30,000 in the shop of Husain Arrayed whose family has been in the pearling business for over three centuries. 'People tried to demoralise me by saying it was not real, but experts agree it is a *dannah,* the perfect pearl', said Mr Arrayed.

Pearls come in several different shades, from golden yellow to white and black (the trade-name for metal grey) and pink, which is white with a rose-hue.

It takes an expert to pick a good pearl from the many qualities. The most important are *dannah, jeevan* meaning rare, round and unblemished, and *golwa* which is irregular and may display some imperfections. Some of the descriptions, like *jeevan,* are Hindu in origin because in the old days the merchants were Indians. 'If you take care of a good pearl and keep it away from perfume, it should last for 500 years', said Mr Arrayed, whose shop is in Sheikh Abdullah Road, Manama.

During the rule of Sheikh Hamed, two things happened which had an immense impact on the life and wealth of Bahrain. In the

1930s, the Japanese flooded the market with cheap, cultured pearls, but before the disaster was felt, the island discovered oil.

Oil and the Economy

It was a New Zealander, Major Frank Holmes, who noticed oil deposits while drilling for water. He obtained concessions for Bahrain and the 'neutral zone', shared by Saudi Arabia and Kuwait, but when his syndicate was unable to raise the capital he left and the concessions were sold to Gulf Oil Corporation, which transferred them to Standard Oil of California. The *Jabal ad-Dukhan* well which blew life into Bahrain in 1932 is located about 2½ miles south of Awali.

By 1935, 16 wells were productive and a refinery was being constructed by Bahrain Petroleum Company, a subsidiary of Standard Oil and Texaco. The BAPCO refinery is still one of the largest in the Middle East, processing 215,000 barrels a day mainly crude oil from ARAMCO. The 34-mile-long pipeline from Damman, 17 of it submarine, stretches across Bahrain to the island of Sitra, where storage tanks and bunkering facilities are located.

First to discover oil, Bahrain is also the first to face the nightmare that its oil is running out. Output is down to 61,120 barrels a day (1975), its wells are given a longevity of only 35 years and it is

The pipeline across Bahrain.   أنابيب النفط تمتد على طول وعرض البحرين

generally conceded that no more oil will be found. Fortunately it has another reprieve in the vast Khuff Field of non-associated gas producing some 224 million cubic feet a day. In 1972, Bahrain embarked on the ALBA aluminium smelter, the first non-oil-based industry in the Gulf, producing in excess of 120,000 tonnes a year. An atomiser plant produces ingots for export as powdered aluminium and ALBA will soon manufacture window-frames, doors and other products which have an instant local market. The company has also instigated moves for the production of petroleum coke for which there is a current world-wide shortage, and if experiments prove successful, Bahrain could again initiate a major new industry in the Gulf.

The impact of oil on Bahrain is similar to anywhere in the Gulf, in that it has created the opportunity to develop its economy on a more diverse basis. But since oil has never gushed in the same quantities as in Qatar or Abu Dhabi, Bahrain has expanded in a slower, more thoughtful way which should enable it to survive when the wells run dry, although this will depend on competition as other Gulf States duplicate its projects.

After aluminium, the most important project is the dry dock, ASRY (Arab Ship Repair Yard), sponsored by the Organisation of Arab Petroleum Exporting Countries (OAPEC). Ten years ago, OAPEC resolved to build its own dry dock for the Very Large Crude Carriers and although Dubai nipped in and started its own huge dry dock, and Iran built another at Bandar Abbas, dredging began at a site off Muharraq in 1974.

The idea of the dry dock was conceived when the Suez Canal was closed and there were few repair yards for the VLCCs on order. The anomaly is that although ship-owners are now cancelling orders, the very countries responsible for the slump are still proceeding to build monster dry docks for fantasy 'million ton tankers'. Three great dry docks in the Gulf can only result in destructive economic competition which will be detrimental to political relationships, but as the Gulf Arabs buy their own tankers, at least they will be able to slip them in their own backyards.

The latest estimate of the cost of the dry dock is £114 million, which is being financed by Saudi Arabia, Kuwait, Qatar, Iraq, Bahrain and the United Arab Emirates, though presumably without Dubai. The contract, awarded to Hyundai of South Korea, specifies a 450,000-ton dry dock, four wet berths and repair facilities by 1977.

Another pointer to Bahrain's effort in diversification from oil and its by-products is the new 8 million square feet 'industrial free zone' located around its port, Mina Sulman. In a scheme similar to Dubai's Jebel Ali, companies pay no tax on raw materials and no levies on most capital goods. The course of continued diversification is in construction, minor household equipment and foodstuffs, of which the main suppliers are the United Kingdom, USA, West Germany, Japan and Taiwan. Much of the food imported is Australian, especially meat, of which Qantas flies in 11 tonnes daily. Australian Trade Commissioner Phillip King estimates exports to the Gulf States and Oman at $A.100 million a year, but considers it should be more given that Australia was the first country to establish a trade commission in Bahrain, in 1964. 'Australian businessmen are too concerned about high standards. What the locals want is cheap, quickly assembled stuff', said King, particularly referring to the unquenchable market for prefabricated housing.

Business Opportunities

Every Western businessmen dreams of a ticket on the 'great Gulf gravy train', but few are aware how local business works. The Gulf is not a region suitable for Western-type market research, or feasibility studies. The power of advertising is also unknown, so that no one really knows what will happen when a new product is introduced. Few governments can supply accurate statistics; even the Embassy in London could not tell me the population of Bahrain.

The most important thing for a businessman in the Gulf is his choice of a good local partner. A big problem, especially for a contractor, is the lack of an indigenous work-force, which means he becomes involved in recruitment, visas and accommodation, all of which can be overcome with the right partner. King claims one of the big faults of Australian companies is their failure to follow through once a contract is clinched. 'It is imperative that deals are constantly followed up. Correspondence is no good. They must come back and show their faces. The Arabs place great emphasis on personal contact,' he said.

Businessmen will find Bahrainis more attuned to Western methods than other Gulf nationals. Although states like Abu Dhabi are richer, money does not buy experience and this fifty-year start in education is the big advantage Bahrain has over its competitors. The first boys' school opened in 1919, and a girls' school in 1928, and having good technical colleges, Bahrain has locally skilled tradesmen, as opposed to other Gulf States, which rely wholly on imported labour. All sections of the community have a cadre of bright young Bahrainis and the progressive outlook of the island and its attractive business incentives has induced many companies to establish their regional headquarters in Manama. In the sphere of banking, this has become a flood.

It is interesting that Bahrain, which always played a major role in Gulf commerce, was again to the fore in creating the region's first 'offshore' banking centre, in 1975. Although the idea was conceived prior to the Lebanese civil war, it was certainly assisted by events in Beirut, which was the recognised financial centre of the Middle East. When alternative cities such as Cairo and Amman were being considered as replacement centres, Bahrain won for numerous reasons. Foremost was the big attraction of tax-free benefits, then its favourable location in a time zone between the major financial centres of London, New York and Singapore, thus permitting simultaneous operations in all markets. Another incentive was its flexible banking system resulting from its association with Britain. Also of prime importance is its efficient telecommunications system, although the sudden arrival of 35 banks put severe strains on Cable and Wireless. They have now bypassed the telephone system by installing a special cable centre in Manama.

Bahrain's political stability has also aided its new role as the Gulf's financial centre. The decision to make it the headquarters of the new Gulf International Bank owned by Saudi Arabia, Kuwait, Qatar, Oman, the United Arab Emirates and Bahrain itself reflects the confidence felt there by its affluent neighbours.

Bahrain has 17 foreign banks which it considers sufficient and has now granted licences to 35 'offshore' banking units able to accept deposits from the government and other banks, but unable to deal directly with the public. 'In theory, but not in practice, especially when an Arab comes in to invest half a million dinars which he plonks on the counter in a plastic bag', said one banker.

When the war in Lebanon was at its height, some bankers were predicting that Bahrain would replace it as the money centre of the Middle East, but barely a month after peace-keeping forces moved in, many banks were planning to return to the rubble of Beirut. In any event, one year after the launching of 'offshore' banking in Bahrain, the volume of business was running at over £3.5 million.

As in the Lower Gulf, Bahrain used the Indian rupee until 1965, when its Currency Board issued the Bahraini dinar. Talks continue among several Gulf States whether to have a 'Gulf dinar' — to circulate in Kuwait, Bahrain, Qatar and the United Arab Emirates, for although these currencies are freely convertible, they can be confusing for visitors.

Confusion reaches a peak in the Emirates where, like the French who still speak in *ancien francs,* people talk in half a dozen different currencies, depending on their age and nationality: dirhams (United Arab Emirates), dinars (Bahraini or Kuwaiti), rials (usually Saudi, but also Qatari and Omani) and rupees, a hangover from the British administration of the Trucial States from India. English expatriates solve the problem by calling the money 'chips'.

Social Life

Bahrain's expatriate population, the majority of whom are British, regard it as the best place to work in the Gulf. The island's historic association with Britain has seen many aspects of life become quite Anglicised, and most enjoy a higher standard of living than at home. Because of its excellent telecommunications, the sense of separation from the home country is not so great, air-conditioning has revolutionised the trying summers, the island has first-class medical facilities and attractive indoor and outdoor entertainments.

Under the auspices of Sheikh Isa, Bahrain also enjoys a freedom not experienced elsewhere in the Gulf hence its residents have a greater capacity to enjoy life. Well-educated and Westernised in their ways, Bahrainis are the most popular Gulf Arabs and many expatriates prefer their company to that of the local British.

For bachelors, Bahrain is the best posting in the Gulf as it is the only place where there are any available women. Three hundred Gulf air hostesses are based in Manama, and the arrival of a new group is anticipated as keenly as New Year's Eve. Manama boasts a small, though bright, night-life which is centred on hotel night-clubs and the lavish 'Juliana's' discotheque. However, entertainment is not cheap. The Union Bank of Switzerland estimates Manama to be the second most expensive city to live in, after Tokyo. A mediocre meal with wine costs £12 for two, rising to £40 somewhere better, such as 'Keith's' or 'Phoenix One', where lobster costs £15!

The best restaurant is the 'Talk of the Town' owned by Sheikh Rashid Hassan al-Khalifa, who is also the first local pilot to fly Gulf Air. For hotel food, the Gulf Hotel is recommended.

Hotels and Housing

Like the other Gulf States, Bahrain has a critical shortage of hotels with a total of only 600 first-class rooms, most of which are booked a year in advance by businessmen.

The tragedy of the local hotel industry is the closure of 130 rooms in the popular Gulf Hotel which was completed only in 1968. Efforts are being made to save the entire building from demolition, a complex job involving injecting the supporting pillars with resin. The corrosion has been caused through chlorides and sulphate impurities used in the cement of its reinforced concrete frame, a familiar story in Gulf construction.

The Bahrain Hilton, which opened in December 1975, is substandard compared to other Hiltons and is very expensive. Two cheaper hotels are the Tylos and Delmon, in central Manama.

Ramada will open in 1977 and Sheraton in 1980, but these will still mean a total of only 2,000 rooms. It also means that rates, which reflect the seller's market, will continue very high and third-class hotels will charge the same price as international-standard establishments.

And even if one has a room, one is not sure of keeping it. An Englishman, unable to find a flat in Bahrain, returned from work, after living for nine months at the Hilton, to find all his possessions in the corridor because his bed was required by the 'powers that be'.

As there is a shortage of hotels, there is also an acute housing shortage in Bahrain, which has only recently stirred itself in this direction. When Sir Charles Belgrave arrived as adviser to the Emir in 1926, he found only a handful of coral-stone buildings with the majority of the population living in crude, palm-frond *barastis*. He describes his own house as being full of rats and lit by candles which melted in the heat, or oil-lamps which threatened to explode at any moment. Cooking was managed on a mud fireplace over a charcoal fire, fresh drinking-water arrived only every second week on the mail-boat and 'sanitation was what is known as the "Indian System" which entailed a sweeper'.

It was not until 1974 that a Ministry of Housing was created in Bahrain. The first houses were handed over in 1976 and a further 2,000 a year will follow for the next five years.

The first major move to provide accommodation at moderate cost for the people was initiated by the Emir, Sheikh Isa, who donated the land for the town which bears his name. The first stage of Isa Town, begun in 1968, and now complete, provides accommodation for 15,000 people in houses whose standards vary according to income. Their purchase is financed in a similar way to a building society with the government underwriting costs which are repaid in low monthly instalments over a period 15 to 20 years.

I saw a two-storey house of four bedrooms, a reception room, lounge, kitchen, two bathrooms, servant's quarters and large garden, for which its 33-year-old bachelor owner was paying only £4,000. He was quite sad while showing me around, explaining that he still lived with his parents as he was unable to find a suitable wife.

Isa Town is too new to have developed any character, but its Western suburban-type layout precludes any Eastern charm. Its

Isa town low-cost housing.

بيوت ' في مدينة 'عيسى "

streets are long, broad thoroughfares, a frequent error made by architects: from Mecca to Marrakesh, all old Islamic towns have narrow, closed-in streets to shade the shoppers and strollers.

It is not a case of coming out of an air-conditioned house and stepping into an air-conditioned motor car, since the evening 'paseo' is as much a custom in Arabia as it is in Spain, which anyhow inherited it from the Moors. Another surprising error in Isa Town is that none of its streets are kerbed or guttered, which makes life miserable when it rains.

Ten minutes drive from Manama, Isa Town is completely self-contained and administered by its own residents who will eventually number 35,000. Its car-free centre is ringed by shops, markets and restaurants, and public amenities include a sports stadium, swimming pool, cinema, library, children's playground, a clinic and a mosque. It also has a public bus service which is rare in the Gulf where everyone is assumed to own a car.

Another large development under discussion is a Causeway to join Bahrain to the mainland. The 24-mile-long dual carriageway planned could carry 2,000 vehicles a day, and would cost an estimated £170 million. The way Bahrainis discuss the Causeway makes one think it is nearly finished, but an Arab aged 76 told me he had heard it talked about since his childhood.

It is seen by local merchants as an enormous benefit to the island, since it would connect them to the new Trans-Arabian Highway and Bahrain could become the major distribution centre for road freight in the Upper Gulf. Given this advantage, it is hard to see why the project has never been started. Expatriates claim the delays are social, saying the Bahrainis feel they would be inundated with Saudis, especially on Friday, the non-work day, when their restaurants would be packed. Another school of thought says that the powerful Saudis, with strong influence in Bahrain may insist the island goes 'dry'. This is unlikely. Prohibition would be unthinkable to the Saudis when they could leap in their Cadillacs and speed over the Causeway in twenty minutes to a legal drink.

Local Life and Tourism

As in the Lower Gulf States, Bahrain is developing its domestic tourist facilities with the construction of motels designed, as a local Minister put it, to suit 'large entourages'. By this he meant the Saudis, who travel in frighteningly large family groups of up to twenty, plus retainers and meat on the hoof. Even without the Causeway, on a religious holiday such as *Eid al-Fitr*, marking the end of the fast of Ramadan, Bahrain receives 20,000 visitors! Most move no further than Manama, although the 250-square-mile island offers many interesting historic sites, attractive beaches and glimpses of traditional life.

Like all towns on the Gulf Coast, activity starts early in Manama, slackening off as the heat increases, ceasing altogether in the stifling afternoon, then resurrecting itself in the relative cool of night.

First to rise are the fishermen, who are seen fashioning huge wire fish-traps near the dhow jetty, on North Road. Formerly they used to drug the fish on the seed of the Persian lilac. Crushed with dried prawns, the 'sim', as it was called, was sprinkled on the surface of shallow bays and when the fish rose to feed on it, they become stupefied and were then easily netted. Today the main methods use modern wire traps and the traditional palm-frond enclosures staked out like fences in the sea.

The discovery of oil has had an almost fatal impact on fishing and boat-building in Bahrain as many men have left the trade for the higher wages at BAPCO and ALBA. Only twenty of the dhows still fishing are reckoned to be Bahraini, the remainder coming from Pakistan and the Lower Gulf.

Next to rise are the shop-keepers in the *souq*, which runs off Bab al-Bahrain Road. Usually Indian and Pakistani, they arrange a web of saris, tools and toys in the doorways, then squat like spiders in the depths. Desultory wanderings through the *souq*, or bazaar, are usually a delight in an Eastern clime, but in Manama's market it is a struggle along crowded, rubbish-stewn streets. There is some colour in the occasional dusty antique shop whose owner puffs on a hookah outside, since there is no room within amongst the mess.

There are few typical souvenirs of a visit to Bahrain beyond pearls, model dhows and handturned pottery. Bahrain once boasted two colonies of artisans, the potters of A'Ali and the weavers of Abu Saiba. Today, only one potter and four weavers remain since, like the fishermen and boat-builders, the 'oil generation' has taken up more lucrative trades.

One sees the kilns of A'ali smoking like small volcanoes on the horizon, some 12 miles from Manama. Surrounded by the graves of Dilmun, many are actually built inside the burial mounds, the smoke escaping through an upper niche. One houses 48-year-old Abdul Hossain, who stands at waist level in a pit, squeezing and moulding red clay on a spinning wheel, transforming it into the type of amphora described in the Bible. 'It was a family tradition for centuries, but today I am the only one left; it's the oil, you know,' he told me.

North of A'Ali, near the small settlement of Abu Saiba, two wizened old weavers still work the looms of their forefathers. 'When

Jaussem Salman, the weaver.   جويسم سلمان

I was a boy, there used to be 300 weavers, but today the young men go away,' said Jaussem Salman, who thought he was about 72. He got up from the loom inside a stuffy *barasti* to come out and show me the red and black textile he was weaving on a five-metre warp. 'The young folk buy their clothes in those fancy shops in Manama,' he said. 'All we sell are a few rugs to the Saudis.'

An interesting stop on the north coast is the cool oasis of the Budaiya Agricultural Research Farm, which was founded by Sir Charles Belgrave. It is laid out with trees and climbers from Australia and India and its experiments involve testing new strains of plants and educating the farmers in irrigation methods.

Although Bahrain has ample bore-water, it has a high salinity content, with the result that farmers tend to flood their crops, which causes a strain on the wells. The steady Australian 'drip irrigation' method has been found most effective.

While southern Bahrain is an ugly landscape of desert and limestone glomerate, the north is relatively green, with date plantations and lucerne.

Dates used to be the staple crop. The great August harvest was likened to the olive season in Sicily when hundreds of itinerant workers came from all over the archipelago. Today dates are a luxury; with some 10,000 palms neglected as their owners seek alternative work. Above everything, the headless palms of Bahrain symbolise the impact of oil.

The sea which laps the Bahrain archipelago is very warm and in summer heats up like a bath. The most popular bathing beaches lie on the west coast, near Zellaq, where the ruling family has staked out the choicest spots for their seaside villas, in addition to their palaces at Rifa. Sheikh Isa is often seen relaxing in his villa, at 'Sheikh Isa's Beach', which is reserved for guests of the ruling family. The setting is quite Mediterranean, with the sheikh's white cruiser moored at the wharf, red and blue Cinzano umbrellas dotting the beach – even flaxen-haired children building sand-castles.

An outing for Bahraini families is *ain-Adari*, or the 'Virgin's Pool', a carp-filled spring surrounded by oleander and bougainvillaea. In Belgrave's time it was a donkey-watering hole; today it is used as a car-wash.

Springs abound on the attractive island of Nabih Salih, which lies in the bay between Manama and Sitra, and in many places around the archipelago fresh-water outlets bubble in the sea. Sailors were able to dive down and obtain water from these springs by pressing a deflated goatskin bag against the source. Other springs are reputed to exist off Ras al-Khaimah, the Emirate at the mouth of the Gulf.

An old house in Muharraq.   بيت قديم لأحد تجار اللؤلؤ في المحرّق .

Although the island of Muharraq is joined to Bahrain by a 1½-mile-long causeway, it retains the atmosphere of an old Gulf Coast town, as opposed to the bustle of Manama. An odour of tar and brine pervades its narrow streets, lined with white-washed mosques and the pink- and buff-coloured mansions of former pearl merchants. It is inevitable these houses will be destroyed by developers, as has happened in Manama, but until now the only changes are where their corners have been cut off to permit the passage of motor vehicles.

One has been restored and may be visited. Its rooms feature carved wooden ceilings in fanciful floral designs and the bridal chamber is embellished in erotic stucco mirror-work. Of special note are its splendid crenellated walls and fluted fanlights above the heavy teak doors.

Exploring the silent streets, one sees no Europeans, and unlike Manama, where Bahraini women wear Western dress, here they drape themselves in the black cloak, or *abaya*.

Opposite the causeway a road runs into the *souq* where old Arab traders survive, hammering chests and making sails. Somehow in Muhharaq, a small colony of craftsmen have managed to keep their heads above oil, in the timeless building of dhows.

'Dhow' is defined by the *Oxford Dictionary* as: 'Any Arab ship, especially used in slave-trading; up to 200 tons' but in fact the word 'dhow' does not occur in Arabic. There are in fact half a dozen different types of boats in the Gulf which contrast in weight, function, design and name. The main type built in Bahrain is the square stern, long-prow *sambuq*, or pearling boat; the similarly twin-mast *shu'ai* which is used for fishing and the big *boum*, for long sea voyages, identified by its stern set ten degrees off vertical.

Then there are others, of various lengths and shapes: the *jalibut*, the *huri*, the *abra* and the *baghala*.

The queen of the Gulf used to be the magnificent *baghala*, a vessel which looked as if it had sailed straight out of the Arabian Nights, but was actually of Portuguese origin. It is distinctive for its soaring stern, set with two tiny windows; the world's last *baghala* lies rotting on the waterfront in Muttrah, in the Sultanate of Oman.

Just as sailing vessels from all over the world used to call at Bahrain, so today 24 international carriers fly through its airport on Muharraq. It is here that one joins Gulf Air for other destinations in the Gulf. The airline is owned by Bahrain, Qatar, the United Arab Emirates and Oman, and its story is linked with the booming Gulf.

A mid-flight meeting on Gulf Air.

رجال أعمال عرب يعقدون مؤتمر خلال رحلة جوية على متن طائرة عائدة لطيران الخليج

Originally called 'Gulf Aviation', it was founded by Freddy Bosworth, the flier who inspired Neville Shute's book *Round the Bend*. In 1950, he commenced flying Auster and Anson aircraft to the Trucial States, and BOAC became a shareholder in 1951. When oil was discovered, the airline began playing a major role in moving freight to the various companies prospecting along the Gulf coast. Its F27s were modified to incorporate wide-angle doors to accommodate some of the biggest pieces of machinery in the world.

In 1974, British Airways relinquished its share to the rulers of the four states who changed its name to Gulf Air. That April, the airline commenced flying to London. Today it operates the 'Golden Falcon Service' under the green and maroon colours of its owner states. BAC-IIIs and Boeing 737s fly the 'oil run' in frequent daily services to Gulf coast capitals.

Gulf Air operates VC10s and five luxuriously appointed Tri-Stars on the Gulf-UK route, via Athens, Rome, Paris and Amsterdam. In outfitting these huge planes, the airline opted for space and luxury, reducing normal seating from 400 to 220. All have a lounge, library, shop, radio-ground telephones and wide-berth tables with swivel chairs. With British Airways' Concorde and the Gulf Air Tri-Star, the region enjoys the ultimate in luxurious air travel. The majority of Gulf Air pilots are still British, but it is anticipated that Gulf nationals will take over within ten years. The hostesses too are mainly British and have the world's shortest stay rate, averaging only nine months. This is perhaps understood when one sees some of the passengers, for Gulf Air may often be late, but it is certainly never dull. On one flight, I sat near an Arab with three falcons on his arm, while behind was a sky-flying Bedouin with her tent strapped to her head. 'Wouldn't you like to take it off now dear?' asked the hostess when we were airborne, but the old lady kept it on, all the way to Kuwait.

2 Kuwait

The independent Emirate of Kuwait lies at the head of the Gulf between Iraq and Saudi Arabia. Covering an area of 7,780 square miles, it has an estimated population of 1 million. The capital is Kuwait City. The Emir of Kuwait is H.H. Sheikh Sabah al-Salam al-Sabah, who dissolved the government in 1976 and assumed the role of absolute Head of State. On the occasion of National Day, 1977, His Highness stated, 'The democratic way of life is not alien... in the annals of the Kuwait nation'.

With a *per capita* income of KD3,437*, it would seem that everyone in Kuwait is well off, yet there is an enormous gap between the vastly rich, the very wealthy and plain rich, as distinct from the nominally rich Bedouin and the exceedingly poor migrants who are building Kuwait.

Kuwait was founded about 1710 when particularly harsh conditions drove the Anaiza and al-Khalifa tribes on to the coast in search of water; among them were ancestors of the al-Sabah family which today rules Kuwait. Water was discovered at Kut, a diminutive of Kuwait, meaning fort, and within fifty years the town had grown into an important trading, boat-building and pearling port, surrounded by high city walls. Here, as in the Lower Gulf States, Bedouin migrations to the coast were initiated by water and not, as is generally thought, by oil.

On 22 February 1938 oil was discovered in the Burgan Field south of the city when, under intense pressure, oil burst through the well-head spewing an uncontrollable cascade in the sky. Owing to the outbreak of the Second World War, the first exports were not made until 1946, by which time 9,000 men were employed in what is now called Ahmadi, a self-contained oilmen's suburb, similar to Abadan in Iran.

*Kuwaiti dinars.

In addition to the first strike by the Kuwaiti Oil Company owned by British Petroleum and Gulf Oil, Getty Oil, AOC (Japan) and other giants made further offshore discoveries. The black tide suddenly became a tidal wave and Kuwait found itself earning so much money that it could have paved its streets with gold. In March 1975, its 692 wells were pumping 400,000 tons a day and production for that year totalled 670,918,163 barrels.

An historic chapter in the story of oil exploration in the Gulf occurred in November 1975 when Kuwait assumed a 100 per cent take-over of KOC, the first country to get full control over its own industry from foreign shareholders. Compensation was set at some £29 million, plus the guarantee to both companies of 950,000 barrels a day at a 15 per cent discount for the next five years with the opportunity of purchasing 400,000 barrels a day for an additional five years.

In December 1975 a 2 million barrels a day ceiling was placed on production because of the reduced sales due to OPEC increases and the realisation of the folly of leaving the flood-gate open when reserves are estimated to last only 70 years. Even so, petroleum revenues from 1975 to 1980 should still top £5 billion.

Dame Violet Dickson.   ديم فايلت ديكسون

Old Kuwait

The grand old lady of Kuwait, Dame Violet Dickson MBE, has seen the impact of oil on local life, as wife of the late Colonel H. R. Dickson, who was a retired political agent. I visited 83-year-old Dame Violet, a tall, imposing figure, in her old merchant's house by the former dhow harbour. 'We have lived in Kuwait since 1929. Zara, my daughter, went to school with the prime minister,' she said.

A true old-style Arabist, she banged a gong and from one of the twenty rooms, a servant appeared with coffee. Dame Violet tossed back seven cups before recounting some fascinating memories of early Kuwait. 'In the old days, we would see caravans of some 200 camels hobbled outside the city walls, the owners loading side packs with paraffin', she said. 'Conditions were hard then. Only one in ten Bedouin children survived and since there was no hospital, the mad used to shuffle about in shackles.

'When oil was discovered, word went round that if one was not too proud to work, one could earn a lot of money and the Bedouin streamed in, erecting their tents like a circus round the oil-rigs. I recall one man who brought his wife to our house and when she walked in the door, she screamed and said the roof would fall in.'

'The changes are acute, but the sensible families survive the pressures. The Arab is the most adaptable person, he bends like a reed shaken in the wind,' said Dame Violet. 'Kuwaitis realise change must come, but they are not pleased at the price rises; rice, for instance has increased 350 per cent in two years. However, Westernisation can also be tragically misinterpreted,' she sighed. 'Recently we saw five of the beautiful desert dogs, *saluqis*, with their tails cut off, as the Bedouin had heard they do such things to dogs in the West.

'Me? Of course I preferred the old days when the Colonel, Zara, the missionaries and I rode horses everywhere. Religion and morals ran deep at that time. We would go out and leave the house wide open, but now, with the tiresome influence of so many foreigners, there is not the same honesty.'

Kuwait Today

Today Kuwait is a juxtaposition of glass and concrete and although there are only five banks, their dazzling facades give the impression of nothing else: the Commercial Bank of Kuwait, the Gulf Bank, the Al-Ahli Bank of Kuwait, the Industrial Bank of Kuwait and the giant National Bank of Kuwait whose combined deposits totalled over $1 billion in 1975.

The main boulevard is Fahed Salim Street, whose pavements are

The Commercial Bank of Kuwait.   منظر أمامي للبنك التجاري في الكويت .

protected from the sun by covered walks. Its window displays resemble church jumble sales, although one can buy anything, from anywhere in the world.

More colourful for evening strolls is *Souq Tijar,* crammed with common Western goods, but having exotic food stores selling tins of curd, jars of saffron and blocks of *halwa,* a sticky honey-flavoured nougat.

However, most of Kuwait exudes a common opulence in a taste that has tried to emulate the West and failed. Stark, high-rise residences crown ground-floor commercial premises, everywhere there are heaps of sand, dangling wires and half-built office blocks where Baluchi labourers think nothing of letting the odd brick plummet earthwards. Many cars have dented roofs which is decidedly not from hail.

Kuwait boasts the smartest car-park in the Gulf, a sort of inverted Sydney Opera House stuffed with long, shiny American cars.

'What counts today is money, not breeding', said a well-bred Kuwaiti as we surveyed his city from its tallest building, the telecommunications tower. 'There are three classes of Kuwaitis', he continued. 'the richest, that is royalty and ministers, who do not work at all; directors, who do not work a lot, and the professional class which works quite hard, but most are Palestinian.'

Kuwait city-centre.

وسط مدينة الكويت

Some 250,000 Palestinians live in Kuwait and it will present difficulties when the Palestine question is resolved since its entire civil service may collapse. However, it is also possible that even if Israel relinquished the 'occupied territories', many might not return, for although in Kuwait they suffer psychologically in having no legal status, they earn far more than they would at home. The unfortunate aspect is that the Palestinians, who virtually run Kuwait, are disliked by the locals, who tolerate them only of necessity because they are unqualified or too lazy, to work themselves.

Like Bahrain, Kuwait's original income derived from trading and the pearling industry. Many of yesterday's pearl merchants are today's real-estate agents, sitting under the Ruler's portrait with Indian runners fetching tea. However, there still exist half a dozen old merchants, slowly opening oysters near the *souq*. Few sights are more aesthetically pleasing than a gleaming orange pearl in the damp, grey lips of an oyster.

'Four dinars', said the man who found it, and people squatted about him, passing the pearl from palm to palm in a sort of mini-auction.

'Five dinars,' someone offered.

'Six dinars,' another upped it, as he popped it in his mouth, spitting it for examination into the hands of newcomers.

High-rise appartments in Kuwait.   بناية للسكن في ضواحي مدينة الكويت

On seeing my interest, a big, pot-bellied fellow reached into his robes and handed me a huge pearl, pale pink, like a dog rose, but not perfect like the one I saw in Bahrain. Such men have pearling in their blood, diving to supplement their income from fishing. Another sat apart, selling piles of six and twelve unopened shells, in a sort of raffle. One could buy six for a dinar and perhaps find a pearl, but he was honest enough to say the discovery rate was only one in two hundred.

The discovery that it was unsafe to take a taxi in Kuwait made my visit difficult. 'It is not done for a woman to travel alone in a cab,' a Kuwaiti businessman warned me. 'Some of these Bedouin drivers get ideas about Western women. Many have never even seen their own wife naked as the women keep their robes on, even in bed!'

I asked the Ministry of Information for a driver, but its Palestinian press officer said they were too busy to help me. If you tackle a man's job, he inferred, you have to be one of the boys. Fortunately the Hilton Hotel operates a round-town bus service from its location on Kuwait Gulf, so I used it for my business visits, riding round and round all day.

When the Hilton opened in 1969, there were not yet many visitors to Kuwait and concerned at what seemed a poor investment, the

Kuwaitis were considering turning it into a sort of 'London Clinic', to alleviate their regular visits to England. Today, like Bahrain, the Hilton runs at 100 per cent occupancy and it is not unusual to see some of Europe's most important businessmen curled up in the foyer. It is a good hotel with an efficient staff. The waitresses are attractive Egyptians, often university graduates who have to suffer the taunts of frustrated Western businessmen because they cannot find employment in Cairo.

Kuwait is the only place in the world where I have drunk lobster. When I ordered whisky in the Hilton, the bill was marked 'One packet of lobster, £15'. Strictly speaking, one is forbidden to bring alcohol into Kuwait, but whether one does or not depends on the Customs officer, and it helps to bring him some as well. The Englishman on my left at Kuwait Airport had his confiscated, but a German behind me was waved through, leaving one bottle and carrying two, clinking in a plastic bag.

An interesting observation to be made in Kuwait is that especially after sundown, everyone in the hotels walks about carrying a plastic bag. The Hilton happily serves soft drinks in its 'Starlight Supper Club', to which one adds one's own 'lobster', or 'what-not', from under the table.

'They call Kuwait a 'dry' country, but I've never drunk so much in my life,' a Greek woman told me. On this occasion, we had dinner with two Kuwaitis in a Chinese restaurant and drank Australian wine from a teapot. 'As we permit Christians freedom of worship, so we allow them to drink, as the Bible does not forbid it,' said one of them. How he qualified his own taste for alcohol is another Gulf coast anomaly, except that unlike in Bahrain, or Dubai, one does not see many drunk Kuwaitis.

Orthodox Moslems drink a sweet grape-juice called 'Grapillon'. Others, including expatriates unwilling to pay high black-market prices for alcohol, drink 'Flash', which they make from frozen raspberries, sugar, grapefruit juice and yeast. As in Saudi Arabia, home-brewing is an indoor sport in Kuwait, but it is not without its own problems as when Customs men emptied 5,000 bottles of Burgundy into the Gulf.

The Kuwaiti men I met seemed to have a capacity to enjoy themselves and were often their own worst critics, yet generally speaking, Kuwaitis are disliked by the other Gulf Arabs. Arrogance is frequently attributed to them and Kuwaitis do give an impression of being arrogant. One sees it in their walk, a rather lazy, non-purposeful gait, as if they have all the money in the world, which of course they do. However, this arrogance can be seen in another way, as a form of withdrawal, or cover, arising from a lack of confidence, since basically they do not want to be the centre of attention. Their sudden wealth has meant that everyone is coming to them. Never a day passes without an official visitor of some sort, and this attitude could well be a defence mechanism. An audience with Sheikh Sabah is out of the question, especially for a Western woman journalist, and it is now a common complaint among Kuwaitis themselves that once they could just knock on his door, but today they must make an appointment. This remark is repeated by the Bedouin of Sheikh Zayed in Abu Dhabi; but this is due partly to concern for security, since the death of King Faisal.

I met an American engineer who had witnessed the execution of Faisal's assassin. 'The police stopped my truck and made me watch,' he said. 'The giant Somali executioner struck his neck three or four times with the blunt side of a golden sword, before finally lopping off his head.'

With Saudi Arabia and Abu Dhabi, Kuwait is the richest country in the world, but since the men dress in the long white *dishdasha* only Kuwaiti women radiate *richesse*. Few wear *purdah,* and they are handsome women who wear the smartest European fashions with more flair than the French. Yves St Laurent's boutique stands on a sandy corner of the smart suburb of Samirah, a sort of Kuwaiti Knightsbridge. However, there is no real extravagant display of wealth when one considers that the Bedouin shuffling down the street might well be able to buy the best in Harrods.

Kuwaiti Business

Kuwait makes headlines every time it invests abroad. The biggest single area is in Eurobonds placed by the Kuwaiti Investment Company, the Kuwait Foreign Trading and Contracting Company and the Kuwait International Investment Company.

KIC chairman, Mr Bader al-Dawood, estimates that Kuwait has has pumped \$3-4 billion in the international capital market in the last few years. By sheer size of its wealth, Kuwait owns more direct foreign investments than the citizens of any other Arab country.

Some of its more splash investments have been the Tour Manhattan residence and office complex in Paris, a £91 million move into St Martin's Properties in London, large stakes in Mercedes and a high-flying bid made, and refused, for the US posts and telegraphs. Mammoth investments have also been made in Eastern Europe in a petro-chemical complex on the Black Sea, a joint \$1,000 million venture with the Rumanian government.

Knowing that it must diversify, Kuwait is spending an avalanche of cash, but despite shrewd market studies, it has still been involved in some spectacular crashes, like its £10 million loss with the collapse of the Intra Bank in Beirut. There are now signs that a few Kuwaitis, inspired by pan-Arabism and a greater confidence in the political stability of the peninsula, are beginning to invest in other Arab countries.

Internally, the government is encouraging the essential trend away from oil and associated industries by providing credit and a degree of protection to the home market. However, the home market still relies 80 per cent on imported goods.

Major investments, partially government-financed under the National Industries Company, are the Kuwait Flour Mill, which supplies all the country's requirements, two cement factories, the Kuwait Hotels Company, which owns the Hilton and has stakes in the Cairo and Khartoum Hiltons and a Moroccan hotel chain, a prefabricated building factory, detergent, batteries, soft drinks and furniture factories, and a high-quality printing works.

For business as well as sentimental reasons, Kuwaitis are very pro-British; some 30,000 holidayed in London in 1976, spending an estimated £200 million. It was therefore also as a goodwill move, to bolster Britain's economy, that Kuwait ordered 13 ships from the Upper Clyde, but due to the failure either to quote a price, or confirm a delivery date, the order was switched to South Korea. This would have meant a loss to Britain of £50 million, until hasty negotiations between Prime Minister Callaghan and the Kuwaitis resulted in their placing another order for six Govan ships, with a guarantee underwritten by the British government.

Some thirty ships on order is typical Gulf style. By 1985, Kuwait will have a fleet of seventy-five ships of 23,000 tons! They will form the nucleus of the United Arab Shipping Company which was created in 1976 by the Gulf nations of Kuwait, Saudi Arabia and Iraq.

Mr Nouri Musaed al-Saleh, managing director of the Kuwaiti Shipping Company, describes the Arab's interest in this area as being the 'rightful desire to participate in the carriage of one's own foreign trade, especially when, as in this case, it is one of the most lucrative shipping trades anywhere in the world.' He reckons the UASC fleet may exceed 2.5 million tons by 1986.

Twenty miles from Kuwait, Shuaiba is its major industrial zone. Apart from KNPC's refinery, which processes 40,000 tons daily, the biggest and most ambitious project relates to the £205 million liquefied petroleum gas (LPG) plant which will come on-stream in 1978. One of the world's giants, it will produce an estimated

2,500,000 barrels daily.

Other main projects involve fertilisers. The Shuaiba plant has a capacity of 712,000 tons of ammonia, 644,000 tons of urea and 132,000 tons of sulphuric acid worth KD51.9 million (1974-5).

Sand-lined bricks and asbestos pipes are also manufactured, but if the government is pouring cash into industrialisation, it is also caring for its citizens in welfare programmes unparalleled anywhere in the world.

Social Welfare

As in all the Gulf States, low-cost housing has priority. The brown and white tents of Bedouin are no longer to be seen in Kuwait, as by 1973, some 13,750 'standard units had been distributed to eligible families'. Essentially this means to the exclusion of the 391,266 migrant workers in Kuwait, as opposed to the 347,396 nationals.

The year 1952 saw construction commence on 17 major residential blocks around the 'Old City' of which only vestiges of a wall and a gate remain since Kuwait, as someone said, cut out its warts, wanting no reminders of its dirty, shabby past. This is unfortunate, since almost everything historic has been demolished: houses, bazaars — even some of the mosques. The fleeting visitor will not see any *barastis*, only rows of coloured boxes, low-cost council houses which cost KD5-7 a month to be repaid over ten years. The houses are a dream for the Bedouin, who previously dwelt in tents, They incorporate the aesthetic 'courtyard design' so valued in a Moslem's private world.

Education also has priority in Kuwait, even over health and is free, from kindergarten to university.

The attractive seaside university is responsible for the education of the few qualified Gulf Arabs and Omanis. Male students only slightly exceed female, but there are more female teachers. 'It is generally conceded that women do a better job than men in Kuwait', said a leading businessman, Faysal Suahib. 'Women usually come first in the examinations and many department heads are women who often remain in the job after they marry.'

The consultant paediatrician at the biggest hospital is a 28-year-old Kuwaiti girl.

Prior to 1945, Kuwait had only one hospital, but today there are eleven, and every Kuwaiti citizen is covered for sickness and its prevention. Of particular interest is a Department of Occupational Health, which is being developed to cope with the problems posed by the sudden industrialisation and its associated side-effects, such as diseases in the petro-chemical industries.

Today there is a 453-bed Hospital for Nervous Disorders, which is rumoured to be full of Kuwaitis suffering from psychiatric ailments resulting from their inability to cope with the massive wealth which has changed their life-styles. The biggest hospital is the 780-bed al-Sabah, set in landscaped gardens, six miles from Kuwait.

Life-Style

Unless one has experienced Kuwait, it is impossible to imagine its standard of living. Unable to take a taxi back from the hospital, I was offered a ride with a cleaner driving a 1975 Buick with built-in stereo cassette player. It was strange sitting beside this oil-tank sized Kuwaiti, listening to Elvis Presley singing love-songs. Everyone has a stereo-player in his car as a driver regards it his duty to entertain, as well as drive, his passengers.

Driving is as hazardous in Kuwait as it is everywhere else in the Gulf. A young French engineer told me he saw an accident every single day. 'Kuwaitis like big cars, with no regard for a quality engine, or brakes,' he said. 'The most popular makes are Cadillac and Chevrolet Impala, but they do not know how to drive,' he said. 'They pass in fourth gear, at 30 miles an hour even in a sports car and if they hit anything, they just leave it on the road.'

I once passed about fifty packets of washing-powder, which had tumbled off a truck in a residential district, which were still lying there when I returned three hours later.

Kuwait has about 900 miles of highways, plus a number of reliable desert tracks, since the country is quite flat, the highest point above sea-level being the top of an oil derrick. Petrol costs 0.15 fils a litre and the 'lover's parking spot' is overlooking the fiery flares at Fahudi.

The summer temperature is very oppressive and the humidity is so high that one has to work the windscreen wipers at the 'drive-in' cinema. 'On 4 July it was 56°C, but the radio will never announce it is over 45° as the labourers can then legally stop work,' my friend told me.

No sensible person visits Kuwait between July and September and one cannot do any business there as most Kuwaitis have left. The best months to visit the Emirate are November to March.

Tourism

Like Bahrain, there is more to Kuwait than is at first apparent and an opportunity should be made to see the countryside. Beginning in the city and working out via the 'ring roads', one passes the spectacular 'Tourist Towers' on Kuwait Gulf.

Opened on 26 February 1977 during celebrations to mark Kuwait's 16th National Day, the $35 million towers were built by a Yugoslav engineering company. One is a 2 million gallon water-tower and the others, rising 600 feet high, house a theatre-nightclub and revolving restaurant.

Around the bay, near Dame Violet's house, is a colony of artists who work in a beautifully restored old merchant's house whose *diwanahs,* or meeting rooms, have been converted into studios. Studying paintings by the 'Kuwaiti School', one detects the underlying influence of the sea and the desert, but then there is little else. 'My aim is to record the real Kuwait', said leading artist and sculptor Eisa Sakr, a graduate of the Cairo School of Fine Arts. 'I draw inspiration from my feelings as a Kuwaiti who loves my country. It is only the beginning of my attempt to sculpt a superb statue out of the dust.'

Nearby is the Kuwait Historical Museum, which is dusty and decadent as a museum should be, as opposed to the splendid yet sterile exhibition centres in Qatar and Oman. Exhibited are models of all the different boats which once sailed in the Gulf, but the main interest centres on pottery from the Hellenistic period, stone seals and Greek coins. One stone bears a message from Alexander the Great to the ruler of Karos. Most artifacts were found on the island of Falaika which lies 15 miles off Kuwait.

Objects unearthed both here and in Bahrain indicate close trading links between Falaika and Dilmun. One excavation has revealed a Bronze Age settlement dating from 2500 BC. The launch-trip to Falaika normally takes about an hour.

On the Basra Road, Jahra, 14 miles from Kuwait, is still a traditional boat-building centre although today its dhows have interiors like Riviera cruisers, complete with carpets and colour televisions.

In the eighteenth and nineteenth centuries, Kuwait was one of the biggest boat-building places on the Arabian peninsula, specialising in the Kuwaiti *boum.* Medium-sized *boums* brought fresh water down from the Shatt-al-Arab in Iraq and big, 300-ton vessels sailed to India and beyond. Usually they carried a cargo of Iraqi dates, and followed the traditional route down the Persian side of the Gulf to Karachi, then southwards to Cochin. Alternatively they sailed down the western shore, rounding Musandam Peninsula, then hugging the Hadrahmut coast of Arabia, south to East Africa.

On the return trip they normally carried mangrove poles which were used for roofing *barastis.* Besides boat-building, the pearling industry employed some 15,000 men, until the desert bore oil.

Agriculture and Fishing

It is amazing to see the desert after rain. To call it a desert is wrong, since it is awash in grasses, thistles and convolvulus. Seeds which lie dormant spring to life along with plagues of vipers, scorpions and other resurrected insects when the desert lives, albeit briefly.

Oil has bought water for Kuwait, which no longer arrives by *boum*, but is distilled at the rate of 50 million gallons daily.

Natural water is available at Jahra, where a limited amount of agriculture has always gone on, but farming faces the same problems as elsewhere along the Gulf — aridity, excessive heat and a lack of water. Of all the Gulf States, this is most acute in Kuwait and Qatar.

Only 5 per cent of the country is suitable for farming of which only 1 per cent is currently under cultivation. The other hurdle is that the Gulf Arabs are not farmers; one cannot imagine today's Kuwaiti shearing a sheep, yet yesterday he must have done so, which is yet another social transition provoked by oil.

Urbanisation has also reduced the animal population so that local meat supplies only a tenth of domestic requirements. Eight per cent of fresh fruit and vegetables is imported mainly from Lebanon and Jordan. The Kuwait Experimental Farm and local holdings account for only 13 per cent, mainly cucumbers, tomatoes, grapes and olives which are grown in the open and appear to survive the blistery summer heat quite successfully.

'If the Jews have done little else, at least they have taught the West Bank fruiterers good packaging,' I heard a merchant say in the *souq*.

Like all Arabs, Kuwaitis are fond of chicken and Colonel Saunders is a familiar face. Poultry farming is progressing with an estimated seven million broilers produced annually. Production of eggs has reached 35 million in seven battery farms.

Kuwait Fisheries is the most sophisticated operation of its kind in the Gulf and plans evisage expansion to 200 vessels. The Shuaiba fish-meal plant processes 400 tons of the average daily catch of 10,000 tons.

Kuwaiti fishing trawlers may soon be seen off Australia, for with Japanese investment in the United Fisheries Company of Kuwait, the fleet is no longer confining itself to the Gulf, but is sailing as far afield as Senegal and New Guinea. As part of its development aid programme, Kuwait has made loans to South Korea and Malaysia, to strengthen their own fishing industries.

Kuwait is not only reputed for its billion-pound splurges in overseas properties, but for its massive loans made through the Kuwait Fund for Arab Economic Development, founded in 1961 to assist Arab and other developing countries to bolster their economies, through financial and technical assistance. Paid-up capital exceeds KD328 million.

Priority is given to projects having direct impact on development and, according to the 1974-5 annual report, some allocations made were ten loans totalling KD41.6 million to Jordan, Egypt, Morocco, Tunisia and North Yemen. KD4.2 million at a low, 0.5 per cent interest rate was lent to finance the great Abyan Delta project, in the People's Democratic Republic of Yemen.

It is intimated that the fund is a means of ensuring Kuwait's protection, in the event of renewed Iraqi aggression, by those countries to whom it has granted loans. Whatever its motives, Kuwait also gives away 8 per cent of its GNP as foreign aid, roughly £600 million since 1974, and more was promised at the 1977 Afro-Arab Cairo Summit Meeting.

Once, Kuwait practised a form of democratic government. The Emir, Sheikh Sabah al-Salam al-Sabah appointed the Prime Minister, al-Sabah, who appointed the Ministers: Deputy Premier, al-Sabah, Interior and Defence Minister, al-Sabah, Social Affairs and Labor Minister, al-Sabah, Foreign Affairs Minister, al-Sabah, who were responsible to a 50-member National Assembly, elected by adult male suffrage.

On 29 August 1976, Sheikh Sabah dissolved the assembly, claiming it had 'exploited democracy and had frozen government legislation for private gain'.

The dissolution of the Kuwaiti National Assembly has left the Gulf without a Parliament, but in any event, Kuwait is more democratic than the Emirate of Qatar.

3 Qatar

Qatar is an independent state which projects 100 miles north into the Gulf off Saudi Arabia. The peninsula attains a width of 40 miles and shares a common eastern border with the Emirate of Abu Dhabi. Most of the estimated population of 210,000 live in the capital of Doha, on the east coast. Qatar's Emir and Head of State is H.H. Sheikh Khalifa bin Hamad al-Thani, who deposed his cousin in 1972, pledging the birth of a '. . .new era. . .of enlightened rule, social justice and stability'.

Qatar is the sixth-richest oil producer in the world, but it was only when Sheikh Khalifa came to power that its revenues were spent on developing the country.

Before the first oil exports in the late forties, Qatar existed on a meagre income from fishing and pearling; today its budget exceeds £580 million. The sudden enormous wealth is an immense responsibility on the decision-makers, mainly members of the al-Thani family, for with vast surpluses accruing all the time the opportunities for self-indulgence and flamboyant development projects are correspondingly high.

Confronted with all the problems of a 'rags to riches' oil state, Sheikh Khalifa is proceeding more cautiously than other rulers, but the pace is rather slow in welfare improvements, since a National Museum, a National Theatre, a National Library and a 40,000-seat National Stadium were built before Doha even had an adequate general hospital.

Oil was discovered on the west coast near Dukhan in 1939, but exports were halted by the Second World War. It was not until 1949 that the first shipment of 15,433 tons was made from the east coast terminal at Umm Said. In 1964, Shell began production from the *Id al-Shargi* field off eastern Qatar. In 1976 the *al-Bunduq* field, shared with Abu Dhabi, began production at the rate of 30,000 barrels a day. On current production levels of 475,000 barrels a day,

H.H. Sheikh Khalifa bin Hamad al-Thani.　　　صاحب السمو الشيخ خليفة بن حمد آل ثاني

Qatar's oil reserves should last for another forty years. There is also the likelihood that more oil exists and huge gas deposits lie off the north-west coast. Provisional estimates assess the field at between 40 and 60 billion cubic feet, which would make it one of the biggest in the world.

Thus the state purse will not run dry for some time and, taking the cue from Kuwait, Qatar acquired 100 per cent ownership of its oilfields in 1976 when the government nationalised the Qatar Petroleum Company (QPC) which was shared by Shell, BP, Exxon, Mobil, Partex and CFP. In February 1977 it also assumed control of Qatar Gas Company.

Businessmen who visited Qatar four or five years ago are amazed at the transformation of Doha's traditional dhow harbour. Born from the maritime trade, all the Gulf coast towns border beautiful bays which are being developed as showpieces by their rulers. Doha Bay affords striking contrasts in the few remaining dhows moored in the shadow of spectacular government buildings lining the waterfront: the Ministry of the Exterior, the Chamber of Commerce and the shimmering gold-faced Qatari Monetary Agency.

But, although like Abu Dhabi, Doha has endless land on which to expand, it dredges new land from the seafront. 'The sheikh has an eye for neatness and the main reason the land is reclaimed is to clean up this dirty, rather odorous bay at low tide,' said the ruler's technical adviser, Englishman John Lockebie.

There are other reasons too. The sheikhs are loath to sell the government their town-area property and land reclamation is a means of government spending. Like the other wealthy Gulf States of Abu Dhabi and Kuwait, Qatar is in the happy position of never being able to spend its entire budget on the domestic economy.

Development Projects

The most ambitious project in the West Bay Development Area is the creation of a self-contained 'space-age' suburb, built on reclaimed land. The complex will provide residential quarters for 'senior staff', a conference centre, shops and a 350-bed 'pyramid-style' hotel. The focal point will be an offshore tower which will have a marina and high-level restaurants.

At the eastern end of the bay is the *emiri diwan,* or working palace of the ruler. Its fancifully designed domes and columns are shades of pink, white and aqua, matching the Clock-Tower opposite.

At the other end of the corniche is the National Museum designed by Michael Rice Associates of London. Formerly the palace of Sheikh Isa's grandfather, it consists of a group of houses which have been restored to their pristine state. The museum's audio-visual exhibitions provide a comprehensive view of Qatar's history, the story of the discovery of oil and the resultant disappearing ways of life of its Bedouin population. Aware that much of Qatar's past would inevitably be destroyed in development projects, the sheikh ordered the museum so that future generations could see how their ancestors lived. This is not, however, comparable to the actual preservation of major historic sites. One day the Gulf Arabs will regret they did not preserve more of their heritage, but having lived for so long in the past, they are as yet unable to grasp its significance. There are plans to save Doha's few remaining merchant houses, but the destruction of Wakrah is complete. Formerly one of the most charming old fishing towns in the Gulf, it has literally been bulldozed off the map. When I visited it in November 1975, its elegant coral-stone houses lay in rubble as if it had suffered an earthquake. The most attractive features of their design were the intricately carved inner walls which were filled with a plaster screen which moulded intricate geometric patterns, known as *naqsh.*

In the name of progress, everything has now been demolished and the first new lost-cost houses are being built on the village outskirts. Each is entered through common metal doors which have replaced the beautiful, brass-studded, wooden ones.

An old fishermen told me that his house had been in the family for ten generations and that it had never once let in a drop of rain. The house had been demolished six months previously and he was living with relatives while waiting for a new one. 'It is who you know which depends on what you receive, although they say that no one ever goes wanting,' he said.

Major problems inhibit the redevelopment of central Doha, which is an ugly face behind the glamorous mask of West Bay. The reasons

The destruction of Wakrah.

for its derelict state are twofold, primarily the enormous cost of rebuilding an entire town and the problem of payment to periphery property-owners. Whereas efficient planning laws regulate developments in the West, here it is still enmeshed in tradition.

Most Qataris have access to the ruler, either through the family, or the traditional *majlis*, and in the event of a property dispute, they can exert heavy pressure on him.

Business and Investment

Property is unbelievably expensive in Doha, with its shabby *souq* reckoned equivalent in value to London's West End. Neither is there any control on land prices. Real-estate values have risen 500 per cent in the past five years which, coupled with building shortages, has caused rent increases of up to 1,000 per cent. There is no longer any rational basis for rents in Doha where it is impossible to find a three-bedroom furnished house for less than £1,000 a month. One Arab ambassador seeking appropriate accommodation was quoted £5,000 a month and an Englishman who planned to buy a house, but changed his mind and decided to rent it, was told that the price would be the same!

The acute shortage of accommodation, prevalent everywhere in the Gulf, is exacerbated in Qatar. Most places are packed with government employees. It is a vicious circle. The government needs skilled employees, but it cannot provide housing — something to remember if one is contemplating employment in Qatar. The Doha Palace Hotel is filled with unhappy foreigners who had been promised accommodation in their contracts.

There are said to be more expatriates in Qatar than in any other Gulf State. The majority are British, French, Italian and Japanese, with the usual numbers of migrant labourers from the Indian subcontinent. It is generally accepted that of the estimated total population of 180,000 only some 68,000 are Qataris.

There are perks in working for the government as George Owen, an Australian expatriate, described: 'Anyone employed by the government requests an advance as soon as he arrives as your salary takes about two bloody months to reach the computer. And if you work for the government, they lend you QR10,000* to buy a car. Then they give you a car allowance to repay the loan, so that when you leave, you can flog the car and pocket the dough. Mind you, one or two *shamals* and all the paint is scratched off.'

No matter when one visits Qatar, it is hot enough to cook *shish kebabs* on the streets. The hottest period is May to October, when the country is frequently battered by the searing, sand-laden *shamal*.

As in Kuwait, businessmen should avoid visiting Qatar during this period as, apart from the heat, it shares the Gulf habit of a 2-3 month migration of nationals to London, Paris and Geneva.

Ramadan should also be avoided since most Qataris are Wahibi Moslems who observe the 28-day fast, which is quite exhausting in this climate. Otherwise, Qataris are charming people to do business with, displaying none of the arrogance of Kuwait, or the roughness of the Emirates, but patience is a useful asset.

As elsewhere in the Gulf, business meetings are held on a low-key basis with Arab customs consuming most of the time. One should not plunge into an immediate sales pitch and never appear to be in a hurry, even though one's expenses amount to nearly £100 a day. Many contracts are lost through business being rushed and, as in Bahrain, great emphasis is placed on personal contact with even an elementary knowledge of Arabic an advantage.

English exports to Qatar in the first six months of 1976 totalled £44 million with the British Ambassador reporting an ever-increasing interest by UK businessmen. The biggest competitor is Japan.

*Qatari rials.

Qatar welcomes foreign investment which requires a Qatari partner who holds 51% of the shares. In special instances, the government may wish to subscribe when equipment may often be imported exempt from tax. There is no personal taxation.

The best markets in Qatar are in prefabricated houses and anything related to construction, furnishings and electrical fittings, a situation found throughout the Gulf.

As in the other Gulf States, the bulk of local expenditure is by the government, under Sheikh Khalifa and his family, who hold the key portfolios.

The management of Qatar's reserves is entrusted to an Investment Board which is headed by the Emir's son, Sheikh Abdul Aziz bin-Khalifa, who is also the Minister of Finance and Petroleum.

Although the regal hierarchy of some three hundred sheikhs is interested in acquiring many of the opulent conveniences of the West, enormous industrial schemes and social welfare programmes have been implemented by Sheikh Khalifa. Many Third World countries have also received loans, whence Qatar promotes its image abroad. Egypt has received a loan of $200 million and, following a visit Qatar, President Amin received £1.7 million. The Palestine Liberation Organisation is another recipient.

Introducing the budget, Sheikh Khalifa said 'that the State's concern to consolidate the basis of the economy...on development projects, is seen as being the most guaranteed road to diversification'. The word 'diversification' is heard as much as 'oil' in Qatar, with £376 million of the 1976 budget of £500 million allocated for heavy industry.

Forty minutes' drive south of Doha is Umm Said, designated the industrial zone, where a 5,000-house satellite city is under construction. Its future population is projected at 20,000. Massive amounts are being spent on industry works in Umm Said with one of the major projects a QR1.2 billion steel mill. A government venture with Kobe Steel and Tokyo Boeki of Japan, it will be completed by 1978, to produce 400,000 tons of steel billets annually.

The second giant project involves a £290 million petro-chemical plant with CDF Chimie, to commence production in 1979 at a rate of 300,000 tons of ethylene a year. Branch industries will manufacture plastic pipes and domestic equipment.

In May 1975, an oil-refinery and a liquefied natural gas (LNG) plant were inaugurated at Umm Said. The refinery has a capacity of 6,200 barrels daily.

A new £116 million natural gas liquefication plant will involve the extraction of gas from the offshore fields. Plans also include a

400-metre wharf capable of taking the largest liquefied gas tankers afloat.

The government's industrial diversification programme is co-ordinated by the Industrial Development Technical Centre, whose other big enterprise is the Qatar Fertiliser plant at Umm Said. Its present daily output of 900 tons of ammonia and 1,000 tons of urea is to be doubled by 1978.

Power for Umm Said is provided by the 145 mw Italian-built plant at Ras abu Fontas which also distils 13,500,000 litres of water daily.

Obviously Qatar will continue to rely on even greater numbers of skilled and unskilled migrants to operate these industries, since although training is under way for local graduates, it will be a decade before they can assume control at management level.

Education and Housing

Following industry, education has the highest priority in the state budget. As the former minister of Education, Sheikh Khalifa's personal interest is improving the standard of education. Qatar is reputed to spend more per individual pupil than any other country in the world. The government pays for clothes, books, transport, meals, higher education abroad — even holidays for its students. Its generosity is rewarded in a high examination pass rate of 74-86 per cent.

The long-term policy is to introduce compulsory education, although in knowledge-hungry Qatar it would seem unnecessary. Statistics over the past 20 years reflect the enthusiasm for schooling: pupil enrolment in 1955 totalled 1,000; today it tops 31,000, given the additional facilities.

Teacher training colleges for men and women will eventually form the nucleus of a university, where the initial subjects will be religion and classic Arabic, science, public administration and civil aviation. Anticipated to open in 1980, the £60 million university will have segregated campuses and ingeniously designed separate entrances for male and female students.

The Ministry of Education also built the huge Khalifa Sports City, which was inaugurated for the 1976 Arabian Gulf Games.

Per head of population, it is therefore evident that Qatar's educational and sporting facilities are more than adequate. Apart from the popular National Theatre, others are subsidised by the Ministry of Information.

QR50 million of the 1976 budget was allocated to provide low-income families with houses and for the better-off, advantageous terms to acquire their own homes. The Government grants free land plus a loan to build, to be repaid between 20 and 25 years. Further loans are granted for furnishings. But in practice, the majority of houses are provided free, since any citizen regularly repaying 80 per cent of his loan is exempt from the balance.

On his first day as Emir, Sheikh Khalifa waived all remaining instalments owned by 'popular housing' owners in a sort of 'accommodation amnesty'.

Unfortunately many of the new 'villa-type' homes are unsuited to Qatar's climate when 120°F temperatures prevail for months. The style suited to such an environment is the traditional 'courtyard design', which keeps the buildings 'cool' in summer and warm in winter. It also relates external surroundings to internal spaces. Such houses are easily maintained and climbing plants do well; by planting even a couple of trees, the temperature can be reduced by 5 degrees. A reduced external surface also logically reduces the interior temperature. Therefore the construction material should be very smooth, so as not to attract dust, which mars its cooling effectiveness.

Contrary to an Englishman's nightmare of his property being zoned by the department of main roads, one of the kindest things one can do for a Qatari is to lay a highway across his land because of the enormous amount he receives as compensation!

Communications

There are no communications problems in Qatar, where the flat terrain is ideal for road-building. Road construction is a continual process with emphasis on expanding the existing links to double carriageways.

Currently there are some 500 miles of metalled roads in Qatar, from where it will soon be possible to drive, via Saudi Arabia, Kuwait, Iraq, and Jordan over the bridge on the Bosphorus, to Europe and the English Channel.

Trucks transporting high-value and bulk freight unsuitable for air cargo will be able to make the trip in 12 to 21 days, depending on hold-ups in Turkey. Meanwhile work continues on the southern road link to Abu Dhabi which, once complete, will mean that one will be able to drive on a sealed road from the English Channel to Oman.

It is a local joke that when Qatar's new airport is complete, that planes will be able to taxi all the way from Qatar to Oman, via all the new airports in the United Arab Emirates.

A prize landmark in Doha is its smart broadcasting station, whose high-frequency transmitter enables evening programmes to be heard as far away as London.

Television and radio traffic, as well as an initial 30 international telephone circuits, are carried on the earth station, which is beamed off the Indian Ocean satellite, 21,000 miles above the earth.

Doha's fully automatic telephone exchange has 16,200 lines, but businessmen should still book trunk calls in advance of normal waiting time as the 'Gulf connection' is always crammed.

As part of playing host to the delegates attending the December 1976 OPEC Conference, Qatar offered a free telephone service to anywhere in the world. Qatar's lavish hospitality to the oil Ministers was another attempt to gain international recognition for the small sheikhdom. Reporting on the forthcoming meeting, even a London *Sunday Times* editorial had OPEC convening in Dhofar, the remote southern province of Oman!

Hotels

The OPEC meeting was held in the luxurious Gulf Hotel which overlooks West Bay. The 120-room, 24-suite Gulf is one of the best hotels in the Gulf and the only place in Qatar where one can obtain a drink.

Descended from tribes in Saudi Arabia, most Qataris are Sunni Moslems of the extreme Wahibi sect who regard exact obedience to the Koran as their moral code. Among other strict disciplines, they are therefore not supposed to drink and the government's progressive attitude is illustrated by its permitting facilities for Christians at the Gulf Hotel.

With the adjacent Oasis and the centrally located New Doha Palace, the Gulf is one of three hotels in Qatar. Highly recommended, it has a Reuters Monitoring Service, an elegant dinner restaurant and serves a splendid midday smorgasbord in a dining-room overlooking the swimming-pool.

Agriculture and Wild Life

Stray camels cause many serious road accidents in Qatar. Expatriates joke of daubing them with luminous paint, but only signs indicate their presence and, like kangaroos in Australia, camels crossing have the right of way.

Qatar's 1974 livestock census showed 5,616 head of cattle, 36,380 head of sheep, 8,148 camels, 42,315 goats — minus six my driver killed on the road to al-Ruwais — and 68,600 poultry.

At Umm Qarah Poultry Farm, 30 miles north of Doha, it is planned to raise 1 million chickens and to produce 10 million eggs annually or about 80 per cent of local needs.

A start was made in October 1975 when 15,000 day-old chicks were imported from Lebanon. When I expressed an interest in seeing the farm, I was told that all the chickens had died, but later reports had them flourishing which, to the uninitiated, is just one of the difficulties of gaining accurate information in the Gulf.

In 1974, 25,520 tons of fodder, mainly lucerne was grown on 110 acres irrigated by bore-water, on the Saudi Arabian border. The plan is to start sheep-raising here and 320 Australian Friesian calves are the foundation of the new Milk Society of Qatar.

Plans are now afoot to inject new life into the old north coast fishing town of al-Ruwais, to transform a dying industry into a commercial business. At present an air of melancholy and an odour of rotting fish hangs over the village which seems to be suspended in a sort of nautical vacuum. As in Wakrah, its old mansions have been flattened and new houses built around the bay where the carcasses of sharks and rays wash in a strange, Pernod-coloured water.

South of here is the former fishing community of al-Arish. Before the discovery of oil, its population numbered several thousand; today only four families remain, the rest having moved to Doha.

Inland from here is the great *Qalat Marir* fortress, which was built when the al-Khalifas settled in nearby Zubara. The desert climate has kept it in excellent repair and today it is occupied by the army.

Qalat Marir fortress. قلعة مرير

The fort's commander offered us coffee and asked us to stay, saying the best *hamour* in the Gulf are caught off this coast. Apart from fishing, there is nothing to do, although down at Dukhan, oil-men have hacked out the world's ugliest golf-course from the brown oil-stained sand.

As in Bahrain and Oman, the biggest commercial fishing enterprise in Qatar is a joint venture by Ross Seafoods and the Qatari government. Its fleet consists of six 'double rig' Mexican shrimp-trawlers which work at depths of 15 fathoms during the shrimp season, which lasts from May until February. Some 30,000 kilos are exported annually to Japan and the United States. The government trawler *Gazelle* supplies Doha's smart new fish market, which is worth getting up early to visit. In the market one sees the local Gulf fish, such as the *hamour,* which resembles a cod and stalls of fruit and vegetables, many of which are locally grown.

Qatar shares with Kuwait an acute shortage of water. Apart from the sparse rainfall of only 70 mm a year, there are few natural springs and in some places, it never rains at all. Another problem is that the soil consists mainly of a sandy loam which rarely exceeds a depth of two feet. Faced with such extremes, it is unlikely that a Western farmer would tackle the challenge of making the country self-sufficient in basic foods, but the Qatari government has made good inroads in agriculture.

In the mid-fifties, no crops were grown at all. Today, 1,562 hectares are under cultivation and the 1976 crop exceeded 21,472 tonnes.

Tomatoes, aubergines, squash, marrows, cabbages and barley are the main crops grown on some 450 farms. Progress is also being made in the cultivation of fruits — grapes, guavas, figs, melons, pomegranates and 164,621 date-palms.

On the government research farm at Rodat al-Farrase, special attention is given to hydroponic cultivation, pasture control and land reclamation. Assistance is given to farmers in the form of free fruit trees, vegetable seedlings, insecticides and a free tractor-ploughing service.

Most of Qatar is flat, semi-desert, covered with a red cobble conglomerate similar to parts of inland Australia.

Natural vegetation is confined to the north, where the desert blooms after even the slightest touch of few. Kew Gardens in London has named 130 varieties of plants in Qatar, which were sent to them by the wife of an oil company official.

By the roadside I found clusters of tiny mauve trumpet-flowers, others which resembled miniature white stars and delicate scarlet buds shaped like small orchids. Unless one can understand the improbability of anything surviving in such conditions, one can never appreciate the miracle of such plants 'born to blush unseen and waste [their] sweetness on the desert air...'

The few wild animals found in Qatar and elsewhere along the Gulf are sparsely distributed owing to scarcity of food and water. To locate members of their own species, many mammals have evolved extremely large ears, particularly the sand fox, the small desert wolf, the hare and the hedgehog. The great distances they must search for food has also seen some rodents develop long, powerfully muscled legs, like the three-toed jerboa which eludes predators with swift, long, unpredictable leaps. It is able to do so by the evolutionary disappearance of two outer toes on each foot which its cousin, the five-toed jerboa, retains. Like the sand rat and the hare, its feet also have bristle-like hairs, to facilitate movement through the sand.

Only a decade ago, the dainty desert gazelle and the *oryx leucoryx*, or Arabian oryx, roamed all over the peninsula. Today the Arabian oryx is almost extinct in the wilds. The discovery of oil has driven it into the last remote area still inaccessible to motor vehicles, the dry, barren plain of Jiddat al-Harasis in southern Oman.

As Bedouin hunters could be seen from 900 yards, the oryx used to have a good chance of escape in the old days, but as with many things in desert life, oil has spelled death for the oryx, as parties of Arabs riding in Range Rovers, equipped with walkie-talkies and telepowered rifles, gunned them down. A *Guardian* report in January 1962 told how a party of Saudis using 'tommy guns' massacred 16 oryx in the Empty Quarter. As a result, the Omani government banned Saudi hunting parties, but as the borders here are not patrolled, there is no likelihood of punishing offenders. It is to be hoped that as the Arabs travel more on their oil millions, their paths will lead them to the realisation that it is dignified to preserve, and not to destroy.

Fortunately an oryx herd is thriving on a farm near al-Ruwais. It was established in 1964 with two animals who were chased by car until they tired and were captured in nets. As the herd now numbers thirty-two, this shows that the oryx does not object to captivity. The ancient Egyptians kept many as domestic animals. Tombstones of the arch-priest Sabonna, in Memphis, reveal that among other animals, he owned 1,305 Arabian oryx!

It is hard to imagine the noble oryx submitting to a yoke. The males are formidable fighters, snorting a challenge, then charging, head down, thrusting their horns from side to side in a scythe-like action. Seen in profile, it is easy to envisage the beautiful cream and

Captive Arabian oryx.   قطيع من البقر الوحشي العربي

brown-collared animal with its slender, tapering horns being mistaken for the legendary unicorn: 'milk-white radiant, inexpressibly lovely. It stood motionless on the desert gravel, one forehoof slightly advanced, slightly lifted, the head with the wonderful long, tapered horns...'

4 The United Arab Emirates

The United Arab Emirates is the confederation of the seven sheikhdoms, or Emirates, of the Lower Gulf, the former Trucial States, which celebrated five years as a union on 2 December 1976.

The total area of the UAE is 33,00 square miles, of which Abu Dhabi occupies 26,000 square miles, Dubai 1,500 square miles, Sharjah 1,000 square miles, Ras al-Khaimah 650 square miles, Fujairah 450 square miles, Umm al Qaiwain 300 square miles and Ajman which is only 100 square miles.

The President is H.H. Sheikh Zayed bin Sultan al-Nahyan of Abu Dhabi and the Vice-President is the Ruler of Dubai, H.H. Sheikh Rashid bin Saeed al-Maktoum. The UAE Supreme Council of the seven Emirs is responsible for federal education, health, social welfare, foreign affairs and defence.

Its budget in 1976 was DH4,151,968,000*, of which more than 80 per cent was contributed by Abu Dhabi, not only because of its massive petroleum revenues, but through the extreme generosity of Sheikh Zayed.

The 1971 British withdrawal from the Lower Gulf came as something as a shock for the Emirates. Having been fostered by Britain since the 'Perpetual Maritime Treaty' in 1853 they were ill-equipped for independence. Federation was seen as the only way to maintain security.

After five years the union is still crystallising, since the UAE faces enormous problems in its harsh, uncompromising climate, a scattered and largely illiterate population, vastly dissimilar levels of development between the 'oil-haves' and the 'have-nots', and the lack of a cohesive development plan. Another barrier to solidarity is the continued rivalry between rulers over boundaries, the destructive economic competition within the union itself and the 'monuments

*Dirhams

race', which reaches a climax in the Lower Gulf. However, the UAE needs more time to mature; also a seven-state union, Australia at first found federation an unruly child.

In 1975, UAE oil reserves were estimated at 20,000 billion barrels, and on current production rates the fields are given a longevity of three decades.

The total population of the UAE is estimated at 655,937, of which three-quarters are foreign migrants, primarily from the Indian sub-continent.

In his speech marking the fifth anniversary of the union on 2 December 1976, Sheikh Zayed said: 'Unity is a dream that symbolises a better life for the coming generations...and the great achievements in construction and development would not have been possible, but for federation.'

ABU DHABI

Abu Dhabi's gross national income of roughly £3.5 billion gives it the highest *per capita* income in the world, but as a member of the federation of seven Emirates, it falls behind Saudi Arabia and Kuwait.

Abu Dhabi is the Western image of every newly rich, extravagantly spending Arab oil state. Before the discovery of oil, except for the white fort surrounded by the *pisé* houses of fishermen, there was no significant building at all in Abu Dhabi. Abu Dhabi island lies off the mainland desert which extends south to merge with the sands of Saudi Arabia.

The majority of its people were Bedouin, the Bani Yas tribes which numbered about 15,000. Date-growers and pearl-divers, they lived a peripatetic existence between the inland oasis of Liwa and the coast. While on a hunting expedition in the 1770s they discovered the island, which they named Abu Dhabi, the 'father of the gazelle'.

Oil

Spudded in on 14 January 1968, Abu Dhabi Marine Area's rig *Enterprise* discovered oil in its first exploratory well, a hint of further vast deposits in the Umm Shaif, Zakum and Bunduq fields — the latter shared with Qatar. Abu Dhabi's main oil reserves, of inestimable

H.H. Sheikh Zayed bin Sultan al-Nahyan of Abu Dhabi.

صاحب السمو الشيخ زايد بن سلطان

The Das island oil-base.

value, lie 80 miles offshore. Drilling began in April 1968. Other major strikes were made, and when the first shipment of crude oil left for Europe in November of that year, Abu Dhabi entered the oil age. Das Island, the storage and loading base for offshore production, is life for 2,000 oil men of some fifteen different nationalities. All live in harmony on Das, because, says BP, there are no women there. The only time the fair sex sets foot on the island is when the Abu Dhabi Ladies' Dramatic Society stages a play for the men.

Dubbed the 'Monks of Das', the majority of men are married. Their free time is spent swimming, fishing, yachting, or playing snooker, cricket or golf. Alcohol is available provided they possess a £40 a month permit. An inebriated Englishman I met returning to Das after 21 days leave told me the average amount consumed on the island is 35 cans of beer and a bottle of whisky a week. Formerly a square-mile sand island, Das is today a tangle of pipes and a maze of masts and other machinery.

It receives the crude oil from Umm Shaif and Zakum via submerged flow-links, wells and 30-inch pipelines. From a score of storage tanks, it is then pumped to floating buoys for the tanker intake. The plant handles, 1,600,000 barrels of oil a day.

Cement factory in Umm-Bab, western Qatar.

Big Gold *booms* moored on Dubai's creek.

Ras al-Khaimah hopes to turn the hot springs at Khatt into a European style 'spa resort'.

Sheikh Zayed judging falcons at the 1976 World Falconry Conference. Behind, his son, Sheikh Sultan. Right, Sheikh Rashid of Dubai. Left Sheikh Saqr of Ras al-Khaiah. Next to Sheikh Sultan is Dr Morsy Abdullah, the Egyptian historian.

Irrigation in the desert has produced a lush crop of lucerne.

Landscape in central Abu Dhabi.

Mayouf Salim, one of the many Bedouin to move into the new houses built for them by Sheikh Zayed of Abu Dhabi.

March-past on UAE National Day 1976.

Apart from oil, Abu Dhabi has an estimated 238 million cubic feet of natural gas reserves and the new £238,297,870 LNG plant on Das will slowly harness the flares which greet one so dramatically on a night flight into Abu Dhabi.

Onshore operations are carried out by the Abu Dhabi Petroleum Company which operates the Murban, Bu Hasa, Asab and Sahil fields, and whose current production is one million barrels a day.

In 1976, oil exports from Abu Dhabi totalled DH26,000 million.

For reasons, unknown Umm-an-Nar Island was chosen as location for the UAE's first oil refinery. Querns, flint-heads and other relics from a pre-historic civilisation around 3000 BC were found on the island, ten miles from central Abu Dhabi, but instead of preserving it as an historic site, the government built an oil refinery. It cost £42 million and processes 15,000 barrels daily, a mere drop in the oceans of oil.

The Abu Dhabi National Oil Company (ADNOC) is inviting bids for a second $500 million refinery to be built near Jebel al-Dhanna. It is believed this refinery will process 240,000 barrels a day.

No one knows just how much oil exists in Abu Dhabi. Deposits are said to lie behind the Abu Dhabi Hilton and an oil-slick sometimes fouls the pool at the other Hilton in al-Ain; even its tap-water smells of oil.

When oil was first discovered in Abu Dhabi, its ruler was Sheikh Shakhbut, about whom tales of miserliness abound. In 1964, Shakhbut's share of oil revenues amounted to £1,479,613 with ADMA, BP, and *Compagnie Française des Pétroles* or (CFP) supplying a further £2,774,859, which he insisted on receiving in cash. It is claimed he packed the money in trunks beneath his bed.

Old Gulf hands like ebullient Irishman Mike Daly, who knew Shakhbut well, say he was genuinely frightened by the sudden foreign interest in his small desert sheikhdom. He believed that the obscurity of a cautious feudalism was Islam's best defence against the twentieth century — similar to Sultan Said in the Sultanate of Oman.

'Why does everyone want to invest in our development?' he used to say. 'Why didn't they come to me when I was poor?'

'Despite certain faults, I found Shakhbut a lovable character,' Daly said. 'Zayed and his brothers were always begging him to develop the country, I was in the palace one day when Shakhbut spread his money all over the *majlis* and told them to help themselves.'

Of course they did not, but something had to be done, since by 1965, tribal pressure was mounting for Zayed, as governor of the

The al-Mukta Bridge linking Abu Dhabi to the mainland.

inland town of al-Ain, to replace his brother as ruler. While Dubai was developing next door, Abu Dhabi was deprived and angered by Zayed's delaying tactics, and three of the Bani Yas tribes actually moved to Qatar.

Finally, with British connivance, on 6 August 1966, Sheikh Shakhbut was removed. It was a bloodless end to 35 years' rule, in contrast to preceding family murders. But it was only through Zayed's loyalty to his brother that Shakhbut was not disposed of earlier.

'After Shakhbut went to live in Bandar Abbas, Zayed asked me to visit him and ask what he thought of the changes he had made in Abu Dhabi,' said Daly. 'With his old horror of spending, he replied to tell Zayed that the al-Mukta Bridge was unnecessary and that the corniche development was madness!'

Shakhbut now lives quietly in al-Ain, on good terms with Sheikh Zayed, who still seeks his opinions. It would be fascinating to hear Shakhbut's comment on the 'mini-Manhattan' which has mushroomed around his old fort, though one still sees the odd camel hobbled beneath a skyscraper.

The Abu Dhabi Hilton.   فندق الهيلتون في أبوظبي

Development

Abu Dhabi is town planning gone wild, where a monstrous bureaucratic machine has created a concrete jungle on the sand. Like Kuwait, it has so much money that the government departments can never manage to spend more than 40 per cent of their budgets, which are startling by British standards: DH925 million on electricity and water and DH563 million on public buildings.

The most dramatic changes are seen along what is now known as the corniche, six miles of sweeping bay where dhows used to dump their cargo directly on to the beach. Today it is the *Promenade des Anglais* of Abu Dhabi, where British expatriates walk their dogs and migrant workers gather to watch the sunset.

The bay starts at the clock-tower roundabout and curls around to the Abu Dhabi Hilton which resembles a giant sand-castle. In 1974 the Hilton was right on the beach, but Abu Dhabi's unpredictable land reclamation schemes have seen it retreat further and further inland.

This is one of the many fascinating aspects of development in Abu Dhabi, since the municipality is reclaiming the waterfront as a marina and parks. At the rate the current is silting up the channels, however, the Dutch company responsible for the dredging is likely to have a lifetime contract.

At present the sheikhs moor their cruisers and speedboats near the site of the new Inter-Continental, at the far end of the bay beside the Khalidia Palace Hotel. Driving from here along the corniche, one passes the original Western buildings in Abu Dhabi, a row of peeling flats, the orange hexagonal horror housing the United States Embassy and St Joseph's Church.

'We were only about eight Catholics in those days and Father used to say Mass in my house,' Mike Daly told me. 'One day, Shakhbut telephoned and asked was it true that Christian services were being held in my home? Although friendly with him, I thought the worst had come, but in fact he said, "Michael, you may be a Christian and I a Moslem, but there is only one God for us both. Send for your head of faith, we must make arrangements."

'So we went to look for land. I suggested a spot but Shakhbut rejected it as it was too poor. Only the best would do for the Pope. He then walked out 12 acres along the corniche. "It is yours to build a proper place of worship," he said, "call an engineer and begin!" '

The church was inaugurated by Shakhbut himself, with the political agent, Sir Hugh Boustead, a visiting American admiral, plus Zayed and all the other sheikhs in attendance. Today it occupies the most valuable piece of real estate in Abu Dhabi.

Near the clock-tower, which points perpetually at half past one, are two of Abu Dhabi's best-known shops, Jashanmal's, which belongs to the Indian merchant family which has made a fortune in the Gulf, and Al Manara, straight from Geneva's *rue Mont Blanc*.

Banks are prominent on the Corniche. The usual Gulf group of the British Bank of the Middle East, Grindlays and the Chartered and United Banks are present, but the most splendid is the National Bank of Abu Dhabi in Sheikh Khalifa Street.

As well as masses of banks, Abu Dhabi has dozens of mosques ranging from the mud and limestone conglomerate of the old Great Mosque, hung with one hundred chandeliers, to the gaudy *Majid as-Siri*. Beside the Great Mosque is an equally impressive great white Post Office where rows of professional letter-writers type documents for illiterate migrants who sign with a thumb-print. Behind here is Manhal Palace, the working office of Sheikh Zayed, and opposite, the beehive of the Ministry of Information.

When I first visited the UAE, the Ministry of Information provided me with a driver in flowing *dishdasha* who put Omar Sharif in the shade. Shefi and I travelled ten days together; he spoke some

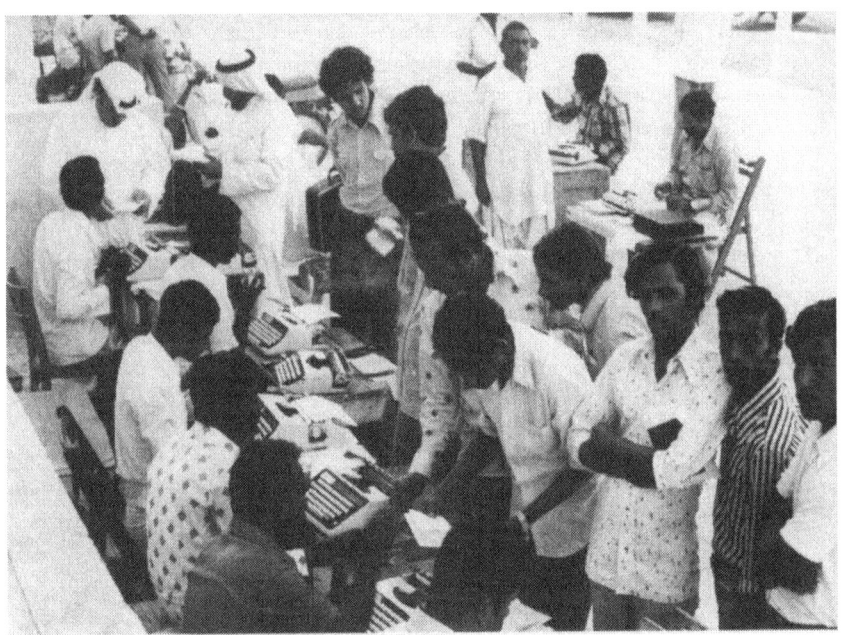

Professional letter-writers helping migrant workers.

كتّاب الرسائل يساعدون العمال الأجانب أمام بناية البريد في أبوظبي

English, had a sense of humour and never took advantage of me. I asked for his services when I returned a year later, but something had changed in the interim. Shefi now spoke good English, which was not surprising as his mind was as sharp as a *khanjar* but his mystique had vanished now that he could converse. Another driver told me that Shefi was one of many Pakistanis who adopt Arab dress in the hope that one day, seemingly 'Arabised', they might get a precious UAE passport.

Abu Dhabi reminds me of a child which cannot wait to open its Christmas presents. It is in such a hurry to develop that there are signs without streets and drivers are forever ducking down mysterious sandy alleys which open one day and close the next, blocked by building materials. Dinner invitations resemble desert expeditions since one has to hoist one's evening dress around one's knees and, shoes in hand, crawl over sand-hills and construction sites.

Talking to any expatriate in the Gulf, one senses a certain apprehension they might be ousted from 'the land of milk and honey'. The psychological insecurity exists for expatriates in any adopted country, but it is exacerbated in the Gulf because of its special bonuses: no taxation; free water, gas and electricity and the national health service.

The best advice to businessmen visiting Abu Dhabi, or any of the Emirates, is to start the day with a hearty breakfast; appointments are rarely kept on time and one's nerves become tensed on all the coffee. I shall never forget one breakfast in the Hilton which began with a hymn and was followed by 'Lawrence of Arabia', supposedly to put us in the mood.

Few foods cannot be bought in Abu Dhabi, either at Spinney's excellent supermarket, or the maze of glass and concrete which has replaced the old bazaar. Although people criticise the new buildings as pseudo-Islamic, all have a certain pleasing appearance, combining both Eastern- and Western-style architecture.

Apart from the usual public works projects such as hospitals and housing, Abu Dhabi Municipality has four major projects planned. The first is a Conference City, in which one senses an answer to Dubai's Trade and Exhibition Centre; but the emphasis will be to make the UAE the political nucleus of the Middle East, with focus on Abu Dhabi. The second is the construction of a French-designed 'Sports City' to accommodate 60,000 spectators for the 1980 Arabian Gulf Games. The third is a National Library, designed by the Architects' Collaborative of the USA, planned as a centre for social, cultural and educational activities, similar to the Cultural Centre in

A supermarket in Abu Dhabi.　　　　　　　　　　　　سوبر ماركت في أبوظبي

Sharjah. The fourth major undertaking is a new airport – aircraft movements in May 1976 were 6,500 a month, compared to only 881 arrivals in 1971 – but since Dubai is seen as the UAE International Airport, it seems extravagant of Abu Dhabi to plan another along the lines of *Charles de Gaulle* in Paris.

Businessmen flock to Abu Dhabi. It is easy to meet with the Ministry of Education or Social Affairs, but to see the Ministry of Finance one must join a queue longer than at a London bus-stop. Those waiting come from poor Moslem countries after hand-outs and Western countries after contracts; and the queue really starts at the UAE Embassy in Princes Gate, London.

I had an interesting discussion on the subject of Western business methods with Abdullah Masoud, a leading businessman whose father was a pearl merchant. Although his only education is from the Koran, Abdullah speaks good English, learned from visiting air hostesses. He works in an office above the Datsun showroom 'Al Masoud', of which he is sales director. For entertaining, he has a penthouse, as any Western executive might; after the al-Nahyan ruling family, the Masouds, heads of al-Maharaba tribe, are the most prominent in Abu Dhabi.

My first question concerned foreigners after a 'quick buck'. 'We

An informal meeting in Abu Dhabi.   حديث ودّي خلال وجبة الغذاء في غرفة تجارة أبوظبي

know,' Abdullah smiled. 'See this man's card. He came in now and offered me the agency for his Texan firm. I quietly listened, but said nothing, since I have it already. Then he proposed me as agent for something else and again I said nothing as my friend has the sole retail outlet for this product in Abu Dhabi. There are so many like him.'

Whereas in the past it was often a case of 'East' conning 'West', today one has the reverse situation of unscrupulous Westerners tricking inexperienced Arabs.

Construction and Housing

Construction is where locals have been taken for the biggest ride and it is a sensitive subject, as elsewhere in the Gulf. A $1 billion fiddle involving consultants, contractors, bankers and civil servants has been hushed up, although over seventy people have been arrested in the first major scandal of its kind.

In looking at construction, one of the main faults is the government's emphasis on speed at the expense of quality. The stairs in the Ministry of Information are crumbling away and a £12,000 rent-a-year flat I saw in the new 'Al Dhafir' building had cracks like

Construction in Abu Dhabi.   البناء في أبوظبي

cobwebs in its walls. Then, when I sought to see Sheikha Fatima, it appeared that Her Highness was busy moving palaces, the ceiling having collapsed on the harem dining-table. Even Sheikh Zayed's Manhal Palace, completed in 1969, by a Scottish company, needs some repair. The Ministry of Foreign Affairs began to crumble two years after its completion and chunks of cement have fallen off the top of the National Bank of Abu Dhabi. Why?

The reason is that in the initial years of construction, contractors threw buildings up as fast as they could and moved out, and the government's own eight-year leasehold does not encourage good building in the race to make a profit before the land reverts to a national.

Stories concerning construction are rife in Abu Dhabi. If one looks at the Al Ain Palace Hotel, one sees the annexe is one storey higher than the original building. The contractor forgot a whole storey and the mistake was not discovered until they found a floor of furniture left over. A British engineer advised that work should stop on building the highest block in Abu Dhabi because none of the cement used met the required specifications and no two cement mixes were the same.

The root fault in all early buildings in Abu Dhabi is that, far from using a special sulphate-resistant cement, even under European supervision, 'coolie labour' was mixing salt-water with the sand. Of course at this time there was no great availability of 'sweet water', but knowing the disastrous effects this would have, no honest contractor should have permitted it. Actually, even if 'sweet water' is used, there is no decent sand in Abu Dhabi. It must be thoroughly flushed of all minerals before it is used which even today is not being done, as the process is too costly. The average life of reinforced concrete in Abu Dhabi is estimated at only ten years.

One should build on the rock and not upon the sand, but there is no choice in the desert. Despite the dramas, Zayed manages to keep his humour and while inspecting the prototype of a low-cost housing project carried out by the Bengal Development Corporation, he asked if he could test the concrete. Handed a pick, he could only chop away a few flakes. 'If I did this elsewhere, the lot would fall down,' he remarked.

This DH473.75 million contract to build 5,000 low-cost houses is the biggest ever signed in the UAE. Built of reinforced concrete, the two-storey, two-bedroom houses will cost £13,600 each, and the order is for 5,000 in twenty months. Two factories have been built where they are prefabricated in sections.

Housing has priority in the budget. A total of 3,418 low-cost homes had been built by the end of 1974, mainly in the capital, Abu Dhabi.

'One can say all nationals are business-minded, even if they cannot sign their name,' said one Palestinian driver. He was bitter as his flat had been bulldozed so a fire-engine could attend a blaze along the street. After two years, he had still not received any compensation and he and his wife were renting a small room for DH700 a month in a house belonging to a Bedouin woman who had received it free from the government and who had subsequently divided it into flats. 'Twenty people work for her, and she owns ten cars, but she still keeps camels in the desert,' he said.

A civil servant I spoke to, Jordanian Akram Khyatt, had his rent increased from DH8,000 to DH35,000 in two years! 'Regretfully we passed a law allowing locals to increase rents as they please,' said Bahraini Mr Ibrahim Sabbah, of the Ministry of Social Affairs. 'There is no reward for these poor migrants who are building the Gulf States, only insults,' he continued. 'They live in terror of rent increases; one month it can be DH1,000 and double the next.'

Education and Welfare

The federal law provides free social services in the Emirates and national assistance cares for the aged, infirm and low-income families in the same generous welfare schemes seen in the Upper Gulf.

Child allowances amounts to a maximum DH700 a month for a family of five and each child receives a financial inducement to attend school; pocket-money if one likes, ranging from DH75 at primary level to DH550 at leaving standard.

In 1971 there were 66 schools in the UAE; today there are more than 200.

Never have I seen so many schools as in Abu Dhabi. There is one down every street and behind every dune and all are the same, white skittle columns and mustard-coloured classrooms, a rather unfortunate choice in the neutral-toned desert surroundings.

'Education has priority throughout the UAE,' said Sharjan Salim Ghamayi, who works for the Ministry of Education, in contrast to his father, who was a pearl diver. 1976-7 pupil enrolement is 73,373. Schooling is free and the science and arts faculties of the first stage of the UAE University, which is expected to cost DH35 million, are due to open in 1977.

'We also have a two-year literacy programme,' Salim told me. 'Schools are open 4.30-9. p.m. with a free bus service from anywhere in town. More women attend than men.'

'The ultimate aim must be nationalisation of civil service posts, to rid Abu Dhabi of its army of foreign Arab bureaucrats,' I said, in his office overlooking Abu Dhabi Bay.

'We need at least ten years,' he replied. 'The first thing is merely to educate, even as semi-skilled.' This brought to mind the numbers of unemployed school-leavers in the West; educated for what?

Industry and Employment

There are few jobs for school-leavers in Abu Dhabi, although the first graduates became the UAE's Ambassadors and Ministers, like the highly regarded Foreign Minister, Ahmed Khalifa al-Suweidi and Dr Mana Saeed al-Otaiba, the young Minister of Petroleum and Mineral Resources.

It is essential that the Emirates develop secondary industries as soon as possible, to absorb what will be a flood of enthusiastic youngsters. Apart from commerce or farming, which do not seem to appeal, as yet there are no unskilled situations and no Bedouin would consider the hotel and catering trades.

All manual labour is performed by migrants and therefore Abu Dhabi, like the other Emirates, will always need a subservient class. Population figures for 1975 of 655,937 show the astonishing numbers of migrants who have entered the UAE since the last census, in 1968, when the total was an estimated 180,000!

As in Kuwait and Qatar, 90 per cent of all manual and unpleasant work is performed by non-Arabs; migrants from Pakistan, mainly Baluchis and Pathans, as well as many Keralans from India.

Arab discrimination against these migrants is evident to all who visit Abu Dhabi, Dubai and Sharjah, where the biggest population concentrations are found. Yet in all industrialised states, a large part of the construction work is performed by migrant labour: the Irish in England, the Spanish in Switzerland, the Turks in Germany and the Italians and Greeks in Australia.

It is easy to react emotionally when one sees these men toiling under the sun, sleeping on the construction sites rootless, and without security. At night, Sheikh Hamdan Street is crowded with them strolling despondently up and down, staring at its tempting window displays. Hindu cinemas offer their only escape from reality. Since there are no women, and Abu Dhabi's 'red light' district was bulldozed on orders of Sheikh Zayed, homosexuality is common, but it can only be seen as a temporary affection provoked by loneliness, for many are, in fact, saving for the bride price at home.

Every migrant comes to work in the Gulf States and Oman, to

Dr Mana Saeed al-Otaiba, Minister of Petroleum. الدكتور سعيد العتيبة وزير النفط والمعادن

Ahmed Khalifa al-Suweidi, Foreign Minister. وزير الخارجية السيد أحمد خليفة السويدي

earn money to buy a bride, a shop, or a farm and although they live in pitiful conditions compared to the locals, the underprivileged migrants do not see it this way. If the Gulf had no oil, they would not be there and the Abu Dhabi Post Office is always packed with tall Pathans and turbanned Baluchis, sending home their registered pay envelopes. These are the lucky ones who managed to enter the UAE and obtain a job, but there are unknown numbers who die *en route* to their vision of a 'sandy Utopia'.

The scandal involving illegal immigration to the UAE was headlined in September 1976, when a dhow carrying several hundred Pakistanis grounded off the rocky coast of Fujairah, a favourite dumping-ground. Scores had already perished *en route* from thirst and exposure, and when the *nakhuda* saw his game was up, he began to throw the remainder overboard. Over a hundred drowned before the police were able to intervene and the rest were deported to Karachi.

Many Pakistanis are quite respectable men who save the current £200 passage. It is not until they arrive in the UAE to find their papers false that they realise they have been duped. Other hapless souls, told to disembark on sandbars, begin walking ashore with their

Baluch workers in Abu Dhabi.   عمّال من البلوچ في أبوظبي .

bedrolls on their heads, only to drown with the rising tide. The Indian boy who cooked for a friend in Dubai arrived in the UAE by swimming for his life.

Both the governments which permit it and the contractors who profit by it are parties to this twentieth century 'economic slavery'.

As it is cheaper to hire new labour at DH18 a day than existing labour at DH40 a day, the contractors encourage the dhow captains to bring in more and more migrants. The racket reaches a height in Sharjah, where I heard of one company paying Indian labourers only DH1.44 an hour and working them a compulsory ten-hour day.

Neither can they leave, as the contractor takes their passports for two years. To go, a man must have a 'release letter', which costs as much to buy on the black market as a return ticket to Bombay.

It is impossible to predict what the outcome will be, but the situation also exists in Kuwait and Qatar, although it is not as extreme there as in the Emirates. It is a joke among expatriates in Abu Dhabi that one foreign investor stood all day on the street looking for a local partner, without seeing one Abu Dhabian!

Investment

As in all the Emirates, investment is greatly encouraged by the government of Abu Dhabi. Investors require a UAE national as their local partner who must receive 25 per cent of the profits, or 2-3 per cent of the contract value and in whose name the business must be registered. Tender bonds range from 2 to 5 per cent of the contract prices for government contracts and 10 per cent for others. There is no personal income tax and no restrictions are placed on remittance of profits.

Major industrial ambitions were announced in 1976 to create a giant industrial zone in Ruweis, 100 miles from the capital. The new city will have a deep-water port of 15 berths and several huge gas-related projects fuelled from its onshore oilfields.

Critics claim the project is in competition to Dubai's Jebel Ali, but it is in Abu Dhabi's own interest to harness the gas, whose current flare wastage exceeds $1 million a day.

One of the first projects is to build a billion-dollar liquefied gas plant to export propane, butane gas and natural gas. Also planned is the Gulf's fifth fertiliser plant, to produce 2,000 tons of ammonia and 1,500 tons of urea daily.

A DH500 million investment by the Abu Dhabi Department of Petroleum and the Japanese steel company Kobe will build a steel-processing plant in Ruwois; for completion by 1980, its initial production is estimated at 400,000 tons a year.

A common sight in the Gulf.   الطريق السريع في العين . أبوظبي .

British goods top imports to Abu Dhabi; most general goods for sale are British and many UK-manufactured cars litter the roadside from over-zealous driving on the four-lane highway to al-Ain.

The second town in Abu Dhabi, Al-Ain is the big inland oasis on the desert crossroads, between the UAE and Oman.

Its luxurious al-Ain Hilton is security from the sizzling heat. After the 1½ hour road trip from Abu Dhabi, its cool marble floors and iced lime drinks are paradise. It is also something of a miracle to lie on a lawn of real grass, with butterflies hovering among the flowers. They can only live inside the garden as the desert starts outside its walls. Since the settlement of the Buraimi dispute with Saudi Arabia, there has been massive investment in al-Ain. Shops and offices have sprung up with repeats of the Abu Dhabi roundabouts, the clock-tower, spectacular police headquarters, schools and mosques. A total of 28 mosques were built in al-Ain in 1976 and the biggest, al-Mutarad, accommodates 3,000 worshippers.

Al-Ain is growing into a fine, well-planned city and some say it may replace Abu Dhabi as the UAE capital. It is anyhow something akin to madness, to build literally everything of importance on a tiny island.

Tourism

Al-Ain and environs is one of the most interesting areas in the Gulf and it has great potential as a domestic and also as an international tourist resort. Its most famous attraction is Buraimi, the biggest oasis in Arabia, which hit the headlines in 1955, when the Trucial Scouts put attacking Saudis to flight.

One of Sheikh Zayed's great political *coups* was to resolve this border dispute with Saudi Arabia in 1974. The two countries are now on good terms and King Khalid visited the UAE in 1976.

Buraimi is everyone's vision of a verdant oasis. Shady palms spawning bunches of shiny, orange dates, veiled women swishing in and out of walled gardens and men thumping washing in its irrigation channels. A leaf from the past and a page from the present, seen in soggy packets of Daz drifting downstream and enormous transistor radios blaring on the banks; not forgetting the mud-walled houses topped with television aerials.

There is a charming little *souq* before one enters Buraimi and the dusty square outside the castle is where slave-markets were held until 1955 when the three known dealers had to retreat into Saudi Arabia. Slavery is discussed later, but technically it is hard to define the word; the nineteenth-century Wahibi attack on Buraimi was led by a Nubian slave.

Tucked inside another Camelot-type castle is the excellent al-Ain Museum, whose curator is Fazal Rahim, a Pakistani. 'They are very conscious of their past,' he said. 'The women are especially interested in the costumes which they sometimes find funny, or merely strange.'

The museum has an interesting exhibition of the disappearing ways of life of the Bedouin and a fine collection of pottery objects unearthed at Hili and Bint Sa'aud.

Bint Sa'aud, one of the nineteen villages in al-Ain, has yielded pottery, seals and arrow-heads thought to date from 2,700 BC. Both here, and along the road to Hili, tells, or burial mounds, are silhouetted like ant-hills against the sky. There is an unusual round, white tomb at Hili with mythical bas-reliefs of oryx and an erotic scene between unknown gods.

It is claimed that only the reliefs of ancient Egypt are comparable to these in Hili which pre-date by 2,000 years anything similar, even in Mesopotamia. There has been little excavation to date, although the Cultural Committee, under the auspices of Egyptian historian Dr Morsy Abdullah, is leading the thrust to uncover the past.

Al-Ain has other attractions too. One is a German-designed zoo, but although its cages are spacious, one feels pity for the animals since until the trees grow there is no shade and July temperatures reach a scorching 46°C.

Ten miles from the zoo, in the shadow of the rugged, red *Jabal Hafit*, is *Ain al-Feydah* National Park where six square miles of forest is fighting the arid elements.

A pleasant 17-room Government Rest House here offers full board for only DH50 single, and the food is excellent. I lunched on chicken, rice and raisins, bowls of fresh yoghurt and barbecued lamb. Regrettably, though, I could not swim in the deep aqua spring, a small point about being a woman in the Gulf.

Agriculture

The 25-acre al-Ain Agricultural Centre, a gift to Zayed from the *Compagnie Française des Petroles,* is an example of the miracle of arid-zone farming, where experiments have shown a tomato yield of 210 tons per acre, compared to 70-80 tons in France and cucumbers at 600 tons per acre, as against 200 tons. Cabbages grown are even bigger and better than European varieties.

When I was received by Sheikha Fatima, her first question was to ask what changes I had noticed, after my twelve months absence. Without thinking, I replied how the grass had grown, and her eyes crinkled behind her *burqa;* for, like her husband, Zayed, the greening of Abu Dhabi is close to her heart. Translated, my comment caused a ripple of satisfaction in the harem, where a big vase of yellow plastic roses stood on the television.

More than anything, Sheikh Zayed is passionately keen on agriculture; King Canute did not hold back the waves, but Zayed will turn the desert green, and at the rate of progress, the word 'desert' may became a misnomer.

'There shall be palm trees and pomegranates, fountains and pleasant gardens...', the Prophet's description of Paradise, is Zayed's dream for Abu Dhabi.

Unless one spends some time in the desert, one can never really appreciate the colour green, nor the Arab fascination with running water, which is why the construction of a fountain is almost sacred, like building a mosque.

As governor of al-Ain, Zayed spent much of his time repairing its ancient *falaj* system. As practised in Persia, a source is tapped and water brought to the surface further down the slope through tunnels. Shafts, sometimes fifty feet deep, are dug at intervals, a dangerous job done in the dark with the danger of the walls collapsing. A convergence of *falaj,* either as wells, or the surface gutters as seen at Buraimi, forms an oasis and all inland settlements have grown up on such sites. Under Zayed's supervision, Awamir tribesmen tunnelled

The rippling desert.

منظر صحراوي في أبوظبي .

The gardens of Al-Ain Agricultural Farm.

إحدى الحدائق الزراعية في العين . أبوظبي .

out the 1,500 yard-long *Falaj as-Saruj,* which took them eighteen years!

The overall *falaj* system in al-Ain supplies the town with 11 million gallons a day, with water piped to roadside taps at mile intervals along the road to Abu Dhabi.

Of all the remarkable sights in the Gulf, it is this greening of the desert on either side of the 162-kilometre road which most impressed me. I made several trips to al-Ain, each time more fascinated by its freeway gardens, watered by men with plastic hoses, way out in this sea of sand, by the roadside, and the miniature forests pushing skywards, fed by miles of drip irrigation tubes. In all, 2,000 acres of trees have been planted; the main species, resembling the Australian eucalypt, is the Jordanian *kena.*

One's first glimpse of re-afforestation is seen driving in from the airport, where 1,000 trees are planted, not for aesthetic reasons as the entrance to Abu Dhabi, but to reduce the searing desert sandstorms which sweep across the island. A forest cover also effectively reduces the temperature by one or two degrees, although this is relative when over 40°C.

Only Abu Dhabi's vast petroleum revenue could pay for Sheikh Zayed's 'green plan', which is pursued at inestimable expense. No one hazards a guess at the cost, but 1,500,000 gallons of water a day is used on the plants in Abu Dhabi alone and expatriates told me the Indian gardeners are so attuned to their job that even during the torrential 1976 April rains they were still standing outside, watering the palms and oleanders.

It is expressly forbidden by Sheikh Zayed for anyone to touch a dead tree. The Bedouin may only use shrubs specially designated as firewood, the reason being they could claim any tree had died and chop it down.

An Egyptian engineer once found a palm blocking the path of a road he was building in Abu Dhabi and, the alternative being a costly diversion, he ordered his labourers to remove it, but by an unfortunate coincidence, Sheikh Zayed drove past and ordered him at once to the palace.

'You will leave the country within 24 hours,' said the Sheikh, enraged.

'I am sorry, Your Highness', pleaded the man, 'let me stay and I will fly in one hundred new palms from Cairo.'

'You are not richer than the government,' said Zayed, compensating him with DH10,000.

In 1969, the government of Abu Dhabi signed a three million dollar agreement with the arid lands department of the University of

Arizona to establish hydroponic cultivation on Saadiyat Island, three-quarters of a mile offshore, in a large-scale version of a similar experiment in Puerto Penasco, Mexico.

As elsewhere in the Gulf, Abu Dhabi faces fearful problems in agricultural development. An extremely low rainfall, coupled with dessicating salt-laden winds, precludes outdoor cultivation on the coast, so on Saadiyat, farming has gone indoors. While cabbages and other crops do well at al-Ain, they are seasonal, and the Saadiyat project aims to produce vegetables when they are unobtainable elsewhere. It currently supplies 25 per cent of local needs.

The plants are grown inside 48 huge, air-supported polythylene structures shaped like half-moons and covering five hectares. The 8 square-mile island has its own desalination plant which purifies 60,000 gallons a day, and a separate system which flushes salt-water over the rigid ends of the greenhouses where twelve fans in each withdraw accumulated hot air.

Cooling is the major problem during summer, when temperatures are hot enough to fry the tomatoes on the vines. The day I visited Saadiyat, there was a breakdown in ventilation and the humidity was so high that sweat poured into my eyes, so that I could not see to photograph.

I was shown the greenhouses by manager Abdullah Kaddas, with Director Mohammed al-Rumeithi, two of three young men born on Saadiyat and especially selected by Sheikh Zayed, who wanted locals involved in the project. All spent twelve months training in Arizona and it is a credit to them that the farm runs so well; interesting, too, as another example of the generation jump, since their fathers are illiterate fishermen.

With the temperature touching 40°C, Abdullah and I strolled along neat concrete paths bordered by giant zinnias, chrysanthemums and marigolds. Carnations also grow well, but flowers are just a hobby, to send to the sheikhas with their vegetables. I was amazed to find they cost less to buy in Abu Dhabi than in London or Sydney. I paid only 10p each for roses, which was remarkably cheap as they had come air freight from Amsterdam.

Vegetables are the main produce on Saadiyat, a different story here since the enormous cost of running the project, transferred to terms of tomatoes, prices them about £2 a kilo. This must be seen as a prestige project for Zayed, since they sell in the *souq* for less than £1. Abu Dhabi has even exported several tons to Beirut, another Gulf anomaly, since most of the fruit and vegetables are still imported from Lebanon, via Syria.

The main crops grown are tomatoes, peppers, egg-plants, melons,

Saadiyat Island — hydroponic cultivation.   الزراعة في بيوت الزجاج على جزيرة السعديات .

cucumbers and bush beans which are inter-cropped with radishes. Lettuce does not grow well during the peak summer, August-September, when only cucumbers and spinach are grown. Despite the ingenious cooling devices, most species suffer leaf-burn, and due to the extremely warm night temperatures, the development of an adequate fruit-load is a problem.

Each plant receives 2-3 litres of water a day from an individual 'dribble tap', to which is added a solution of concentrated fertilisers. As Abu Dhabi's population increases, it is hoped that ultimately only those crops yielding large amounts per greenhouse unit, such as tomatoes and cucumbers, will be grown. Present production is two tons a day.

Apart from the Abu Dhabian directors, the Saadiyat labourers are Pakistani, since the local Kimzan tribe is not interested in farming.

'It is a pity that our students are not interested in agriculture,' said Abdullah, as we combated our dehydration with bottles of iced 7-UP. 'Despite the incentives of free land and seeds from the Ministry of Agriculture, the young people are only interested in quick commercial returns.'

This must, doubtless, disappoint the green-fingered Sheikh Zayed, but perhaps when agriculture assumes greater importance, farming will be more attractive.

A symbolic display of the seven rulers.

Sheikh Zayed

Sheikh Zayed has been accused by the British press of running the UAE as a one-man band and because of his extreme generosity, it can be misconstrued that what Zayed says is what goes, but in fact without him, one cannot see the union surviving.

Zayed works hard for Abu Dhabi, but none pulls harder than he for federation and it was a big disappointment when the Supreme Council decided against adopting a permanent constitution, as had been planned, after the first five-year period.

The union nearly lost Zayed, who threatened to resign but he agreed to re-election providing a financial committee looked into the sharing of federal costs, at present borne almost entirely by Abu Dhabi.

A quiet, fatherly-looking man, Zayed manages to combine the charm of the Bedouin with the charisma of a world statesman.

'He speaks little, but well and like many Bedouin, to make a point, he frequently recites poetry,' said Dr Morsy Abdullah.

No one in need who visits Zayed ever leaves empty-handed. He once flew a stallion to a Dutch boy who had written to ask about Arab horses, yet for all his generosity, Zayed is no one's fool.

A certain sheikh built himself a lavish palace in Abu Dhabi, right down to the old story of solid gold bath taps. Before he even had a chance to move in, Zayed said it would do nicely as a guest palace, which is what it is.

The Bedouin address him simply as *'Abu Khalifa'*, meaning 'Father of Khalifa', the traditional tribal greeting which means, father of the first son, in this case Crown Prince Khalifa. Zayed is said to prefer this as a sincere greeting from his people, much more than the Western-style 'Your Highness'.

And more than any other ruler in the Gulf, Zayed has greatly improved the living standards of the Bedouin. One of my drivers told me that on seeing a poor desert settlement, Zayed will put down in his helicopter and order it houses and schools.

'Money is of no value, unless it is used for the benefit of the people,' says Zayed.

I heard only one complaint about the sheikh, from an old Bedouin in al-Ain.

'Before we could just call on him, now we must make an appointment,' he said.

Zayed's *majlis* is always open, only today there is a queue.

DUBAI

The Clearing House of the Gulf

Unlike Abu Dhabi, Dubai had a sound entrepôt foundation before the discovery of oil. In this it resembles Bahrain, although Dubai never had the same dependence on the pearling industry.

In 1963, Continental Oil Company formed the Dubai Petroleum Company (DPC) to operate onshore concessions which proved unproductive, but in 1966, its half-share in an offshore concession held by Dubai Marine Areas (DUMA) discovered oil.

Dubai's ruler, H.H. Sheikh Rashid bin Saeed al-Maktoum, named the field 'al Fateh', meaning 'good fortune', and the Emirate's good fortune continued when a second field was discovered in 1970, ten miles west, and dubbed 'South West Fateh'. DPC rapidly developed its fields and the first crude-oil shipment of 180,000 barrels left Dubai in September 1969, making it the sixth oil-exporting state in the Gulf.

'Al Fateh' storage and off-loading represents the successful application of an exciting concept permitting offshore production operations independent of the mainland.

The Gulf is too shallow here to enable giant tankers to load oil from an onshore base, so three huge *khazzans*, or storage tanks, are deployed in direct loading from the field, 58 miles off the mainland.

Made of steel and shaped like an inverted champagne glass, each *khazzan* weighs 125,000 tons, is large enough to cover a fifteen-storey building and holds 500,000 barrels of oil. Despite their vast size and weight, the Chicago-manufactured *khazzans* were towed out in one day, but several days were occupied in balancing air-pressure and sea-water volume in the tanks, to slowly submerge them to 155 feet and pin them on the sea-bed.

Bottomless, they utilise the principle that oil and water do not mix, and being lighter than water, oil flows in the top, pushing water out the bottom leaving the *khazzan* full of oil. Conversely, as oil is pumped off the top to the tankers, the sea level rises in the *khazzan*, forcing oil upwards.

However, oil production in Dubai has not been without the associated dramas which are every rigger's nightmare.

In October 1973, Well A-2 on the Fateh Field blew out, destroying its production platform. More serious was the big 'blow-out' of July 1975, which released poisonous hydrogen sulphide gas burning over 100 square yards, presenting a danger to shipping.

Teams of divers, among them the Red Adair 'Troubleshooters', tried every method known to harness the 'rogue well', mainly pumping mud and concrete over the seeping area, which was 4,000 feet deep. It was then left to burn itself out, having lost 3.5 million cubic feet of gas a day, exceeding even the great gas fire of 1961 in the Algerian Sahara.

Nature intervened in March 1976 when, during a violent storm off Dubai, the well blocked itself off, indicating some movement on the sea-bed.

Although Dubai is known to have existed as a fishing and pearling community in the Middle Ages, there are no records before 1833. At this time, it was a dependency of Abu Dhabi, but following an altercation there, 800 Bani Yas moved to Dubai, establishing an independent sheikhdom.

For some time the Emirate was exposed to retaliation from Abu Dhabi and also neighbouring Sharjah, but the ruler, Sheikh Muktum, played one off against the other and through him, solid foundations were laid for friendship with Britain.

A significant event occured in Dubai's more recent history when many merchants from the rival Persian port of Linegh moved to Dubai to avoid its high customs duties. A second influx arrived in 1902, mainly Sunni Moslems escaping religious pressure in the predominantly Shia Moslem society of Persia.

Abetted by the decline of Linegh and aided by the liberal policies of Sheikh Maktoum, Dubai developed into the major commercial emporium of the Gulf and became a regular port of call for steamers *en route* to India and the East.

However, in 1940 tribal rivalries flared over borders with Sharjah when both sides were so short of ammunition that they used to call an evening truce to enable the cannon-balls to be collected for the fight the following day! The dispute was settled by the Trucial Scouts, and under Dubai's present ruler, Sheikh Rashid, who succeeded his father in 1958, the only blasts that are heard are those on building sites, although the border problem remains delicate.

Although his father laid a solid foundation for Sheikh Rashid, it is through his business acumen and daring foresight that Dubai is today the main entrepôt of the Gulf.

Above all, Sheikh Rashid is a merchant, known from Kuwait to Muscat as 'the fox of the Gulf'; even Lebanese businessmen hold him in awe.

'Here everyone is equal,' said Lebanese real-estate agent, Elias Bahou. 'When you come to Dubai, you feel you can breathe properly. Its merchants are honest and since there are no restrictions, trading is quick with goods rapidly resold. Dubai will always be the leader of the Gulf trade, the direct result of the clever rule of Sheikh Rashid in employing the best methods for his country.'

'Sheikh Rashid rules Dubai like a Phoenician state,' said British Airways manager Colin Bird. 'He considers any trade that is good, is good for Dubai and his council is composed almost entirely of merchants. He works hard and is well liked.'

If Abu Dhabians admire Sheikh Zayed, in Dubai they hero-worship Sheikh Rashid and I confess to being quite impressed myself. The Sheikh has a certain charisma, a calm, overtly masculine dignity with enormously alert eyes set in a deeply lined face.

On the federation of the Trucial States many people felt that Sheikh Rashid should have been President, but the sheikh was too cunning, accepting the Vice-Presidency so that he had maximum time to develop Dubai.

A man of ordinary taste, he has not adopted the flashy life-styles of many Gulf Arabs, including his sons. After work he likes to relax on the verandah of his palace, discussing the future of Dubai with his friends. An early riser, he holds Cabinet at 6 a.m., working the

H.H. Sheikh Rashid bin Saeed al-Maktoum.

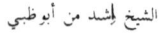

rest of the day in his office on the creek.

Dubai's salt-water creek, or *khor,* is its essential difference to the Upper Gulf States and although Sharjah and Ras al Khaimah have similar inlets, Dubai's creek is the most picturesque. The six-mile long creek has been a determining factor in the Emirate's trading history, since it provided anchorage for up to 500 boats, which used to unload their cargoes directly in the centre of town. Sailors used to speak of Dubai as the 'Venice of Arabia', an apt comparison with oarsmen ferrying passengers from side to side in black, pointed *abras,* a sort of 'Gulf gondola.' In former times, the dhows used to tie up on the steps of the splendid old mud and plaster mansions lining the creek.

The crowning architectural features of these merchant houses were the wind-towers, rising in rows on the roofs. Intricately carved with filigree and plaster-stucco designs, the towers were the world's first form of air-conditioning, standing with open throats to any breeze and funnelling it to the rooms below. Today only a score remain, near the Indian *souq* in Deira and in the Bastikia, or 'Persian merchant's' quarter in Dubai.

Local expatriates are concerned as to whether Rashid will preserve the towers, as the houses occupy some of the most valuable real estate in Dubai. The decision also has political undertones; many locals want the houses demolished as they belong to rich Persian merchants. If the sheikh is shrewd, the towers will be safe, for they represent the last of the old 'Gulf style' architecture which make Dubai unique.

One vessel no longer to be seen on the creek is the big gold *boum,* for although several were moored near the Mazda Building as late as 1974, today's high prices for gold have put the smugglers out of business.

Trade

Many of Dubai's leading families made their fortunes from gold-smuggling, yet as the London *Times* wrote in 1969, 'the merchants of Dubai are not breaking any laws.' The re-export of gold was quite legal, and at one time Dubai was importing a fifth of the world total.

According to Fred Halliday in *Arabia Without Sultans,* by 1970, 250 tons of gold a year passed through Dubai, bringing it an estimated £80 million.

The wind-towers of Dubai.

أبراج الهواء في أبوظبي .

A special hand-size ten tola (3.75 oz.) was minted by Swiss bullion firms, and banks such as the First National City Bank and the British Bank of the Middle East were two of the main buyers for Dubai's gold merchants.

The loser in the smuggling business was India, where gold is regarded with holy significance and in the days when it cost £18 an ounce, the higher Indian price gave the smugglers a steady 10 per cent profit a trip. Returning, they brought in silver, again quite legal when it arrived in Dubai, where British Airways Friday freight was 'coiled wire', bound for Chancery Lane silver vaults.

But if high market prices, rather than Indian coastal patrols, have put the free-wheeling gold merchants out of business, some of the old crewmen remain, working in other jobs around Dubai.

One is a coal-black deck-hand who works on the Inter-Continental Hotel dhow, the *Rawala*. Few people realise that the old turbanned fellow, catching twice as many fish as they, had a colourful career as a gold-runner. Zipped into a scarlet terylene boiler-suit and wearing a huge, gold, eagle-shaped ring, Said perched on the gunwale and recalled his experiences.

Sixty years old, he was born to a slave near Bandar Abbas, crossing to Dubai in 1945, where he obtained work as helmsman on a *boum* running gold to Bombay. The *boums* were powered by three 240-300 h.p. motors, often Rolls-Royce engines, removed and restored from old Centurion tanks left by the British in Sharjah. Depending on the weather, a trip took 8-12 days, the *boum* usually running on one motor, but if the Indian coastguard gave chase, all three were gunned into action, leaving them far behind. Sometimes it did happen that the Indians closed in, when, to avoid capture, the crew flung the gold overboard.

'Once we threw 100 kilos of gold into the Gulf,' he said. This was the average amount carried on most of the *boums* which used to rendezvous with another boat 15-25 miles off the Indian coast and transfer the gold.

'There must be hundreds of millions worth of bullion out there. Hasn't anyone tried to salvage it?' I asked through an interpreter.

'The sea-bed is very soft, and the gold will have sunk deep into the silt. Also the water is murky and there are sharks,' Said replied.

But had he heard of new equipment such as echo sounders, the ORE bottom profiler and other sonic scans which can detect metal under the sea-floor? Spreading his broad, oar-like palms, he said that

Said, the gold-smuggler.

مهرّب ذهب سابق في دبي .

no one really knows where it is. It is all over the place, perhaps billions in dumped gold, but maybe even the *nakhudas* do not remember.

'In the early days, we used to make a profitable 8-10 trips a year. I know some dhows still smuggle gold but because of the danger', he drew a finger across his throat, 'no one knows from where they sail, except that the rendezvous points are much further south, even off the coast of India.'

'There was never any trouble on my boat, but I heard of men who were murdered and thrown to the sharks. Today, they smuggle watches, radios and televisions, but the cargo is always packed in sealed boxes, so no one knows what it contains.'

In Bombay, the Collector of Customs, Mr M. L. Wadhawan, is attempting to break this new smuggling from Dubai by cracking down on street hawkers, even making swoop searches of crewmen's homes.

During 1975, the market value of goods seized was R454.7* million, including one £17,000 haul of watches, calculators and cassettes in sacks marked 'Dubai Flour Mill.' Patrols have been intensified with high-speed Norwegian craft, but while there is a demand for luxury goods by rich Indians on one side of the Gulf and a cheap market on the other, the big *boums* will continue to run the risks between.

Development

The character of Dubai is still very much a 'water city', but the hotels, banks and office-blocks lining its banks remind one more of Hong Kong than of Venice.

The water is the same jade green and the maritime traffic just as busy, the dhows resembling junks and the small *abras* sampans; only the crews are different, wearing turbans instead of coolie hats, and singing as they work, something the Chinese never do.

Like Hong Kong, Dubai has an underwater tunnel which is something the other Emirates cannot copy, unless Ras al Khaimah does, but then Dubai's Shandagha Tunnel cost nearly £8 million.

The cost and length of the tunnel, only 3,000 feet, made most expatriates dismiss it as Dubai's entry in the 'monuments race', but Sheikh Rashid's idea of a submarine carriageway was intended to allow the traditional dhow traffic to continue without hindrance.

With 18,000 motor vehicles registered in Dubai, congestion on

*Indian rupees

A dhow trip in Dubai.   الزوار يتمتعون برحلة بحرية .

the only bridge across the creek became impossible; with Muscat-Muttrah it witnessed the worst traffic-jams in the Gulf. Therefore an open-span bridge was built and a second fixed carriageway, parallel to al-Maktoum Bridge.

Then, in December 1976, Sheikh Rashid opened al-Garhoud Bridge, the longest and biggest in the Gulf, enabling through travellers to the northern Emirates to bypass central Dubai. Its construction was unusual in that it was built over dry land, at right-angles to the creek, whose course was switched to flow beneath it.

Up here, where the creek spreads out into *sabkha,* 25 million cubic metres has been dredged and reclaimed in a recreational scheme of the sheikh's to create islands, holiday homes and marinas. In another project, 150 acres of desert at al-Saffa, near Jumeira, is being transformed into a 16,000-tree park. Its lakeside restaurants are designed by Patrick Gwynne, the architect responsible for London's Hyde Park restaurants.

Near here is the Gulf's most spectacular monument to oil, Dubai's giant Trade and Exhibition Centre, which rises out of the desert like Brussels huge Berlaymont building, headquarters of the EEC.

The £60 million centre, being built by Bernard Sunley, will house every major trading company in Dubai, a 350-bed hotel and a 3,500-seat conference centre.

But these are only the business facilities, for the complex also contains an exhibition centre, similar to Olympia and likewise able to be flooded for boat shows, a swimming-pool, tennis-courts, a boxing-ring and skating-rink. How the Arabs will skate in their *dishdashas* will be seen when the centre opens in 1979-80.

Dubai leads the other Emirates in industrial diversification with one of the most expensive projects its £165 million dry dock. Sheikh Rashid decided to build a dry dock, despite OAPEC's plan to build one in Bahrain, and of course Dubai's will be bigger, in fact the biggest in the world with three yards, two for ships up to 500,000 tons and a third for the 'million-ton tanker'. Work is half-way complete on the dock, being built by Costain/Taylor Woodrow, who built Port Rashid, and have been awarded the £85 million contract for its 22-berth extension. Port Rashid will ultimately have 37 berths and an area of warehousing equivalent in size to the City of London.

Critics claim the port will never operate at full capacity, but in May 1976, there were 58 boats waiting for a berth, according to

Port Rashid, Dubai.   ميناء راشد ، دبي .

May 1976, there were 58 boats waiting for a berth, according to Mr W Duff, Financial Expert to the Ruler.

The lengthening queue of ships has launched Sheikh Rashid on his biggest project of all time, a great 74-berth industrial port and 'free zone' at Jebel Ali, the scope and cost of which are so mind-boggling that the usual critics are still at a loss for words.

The port will have 15 berths for bulk cargo, 15 for transit, 5 for container traffic, 14 for general cargo and the other 25 destined for the 'free zone'. The total length of the quays will be 9 miles and the total cost £440 million!

Seventeen miles south-west of Dubai, Jebel Ali is planned as the centre of the Emirate's industrialisation programme and government plans include an aluminium smelter, a liquefied gas plant, a steelworks, power station and desalination plant, an airport specifically designed to suit these projects and the aforementioned port. The total capital cost of these projects is estimated in 1976 prices at more than $2 billion.

The biggest single venture ever undertaken in Dubai, or anywhere in the Gulf, is the $612 million aluminium smelter owned by Dubai Aluminium Company Ltd, of which the government holds 80 per cent shares.

British banks of Morgan Grenfell, Lloyds International, Wardley Middle East and the Arab and Morgan Grenfell Finance Company Limited played a major role in the Eurodollar loan of $225 million to finance the project for the sheikh.

The contract was awarded to British Smelter Constructions Ltd, which built the ALBA smelter, and management will be by Southwire Company of Georgia, one of the largest producers of aluminium rod, wire and cable in the USA. Other advisers are Japanese, German and Swiss.

The smelter will be fuelled by dry gas offtake from the liquefied gas plant and when complete, by 1981, will process 135,000 tons annually. The loan is the biggest ever raised for a Gulf State. Disinterested parties see the smelter as an extravagant duplication of ALBA which still has some 60,000 tons of aluminium stockpiled, following the slump in world demand. The two smelters will bring Dubai and Bahrain into head-on battle and the crunch may be a disaster for both.

Apart from broadening the industrial base of Dubai's economy, the smelter is seen as a source of employment for some 1,600 people and will introduce new skills to the Emirate.

The other associated plan of Rashid's for Jebel Ali can only be seen as a 'pipe dream'. He intends to create of it a 'free city', where

no visas are necessary, but how everyone will live and work within, forbidden to cross its borders, is a mystery.

The huge new earth station near Jebel Ali is still a mystery to many Bedouin, some of whom have never used a telephone. Inaugurated in 1975, it put the desert sheikhdoms in the space age. A decade ago, as the Trucial States, they averaged 20 overseas calls a day; in 1976, international calls from the UAE exceeded 2,500 per day, which is unprecedented in world telecommunications history.

Tourism

Attempting to preserve Dubai's history is a New Zealander Yvonne Chetwin, whose husband, David, is project manager for the dry dock. She has collected an interesting number of desert artifacts, representing the dying ways of life. Of special note are sharkskin shields and pristine pearl-diving equipment.

'My budget is very small,' she said, showing me the museum which is in a nineteenth century fortress in the Bastikia.

In not displaying an interest in their heritage, the Dubai Arabs are no different to others. Only when their culture nearly dies will they rouse themselves to conservation.

Some 8,000-12,000 expatriates are estimated to be working in the UAE, mainly in Abu Dhabi, Sharjah and Dubai. Of this figure, two or three thousand, chiefly British and American, live in Dubai. The flight from London to Dubai takes about seven hours.

The three-mile taxi trip from Dubai Airport to the business centre in Deira costs DH20. Deira is the best shopping centre in the Gulf. Its modern stores sell everything an expatriate requires to furnish a house, although inflation over the last three years has seen big price increases; once Dubai was almost as cheap as Hong Kong.

The main Western-type shopping area extends along the creek from the Inter-Continental Hotel to the Juma al-Majid Building. Farther down, the Indians take over in a sort of 'mini Bombay' without the beggars.

An odour of curry drifts from the cafes and incense from the shops, selling all manner of gaudy bric-a-brac from the Indian subcontinent. Indians and Pakistanis also monopolise shops in the shadowy old gold *souq*, which is under demolition order for replacement by a modern shopping complex.

Yvonne Chetwin, curator of Dubai Museum.

إيفون حتوين مديرة متحف دبي .

Investment

Although Dubai was prosperous before federation, it has shot even further ahead with the added stability as a member of the UAE. Prior to this, there was no massive investment there, but today a great confidence is felt in Dubai from abroad, seen in the construction of some of the world's top hotel chains: Sheraton, Hyatt and Inter-Continental. The Dubai Inter-Continental is the first of seven to be built in the Gulf, the chain's biggest investment in any one region. Opened in 1975 on the creekside in Deira, the luxury Inter-Continental has suffered the same fate as Abu Dhabi's Hilton.

Sheikh Rashid has reclaimed land in front of it to create a corniche where 18,000 people will live in a French-designed 'mini-city' of hotels, office blocks, apartments, schools, mosques. There is even a zoo.

Happily, the 'Panorama Cocktail' lounge of the Inter-Continental cannot be built out and remains the most romantic spot for a sundowner in the Gulf.

The 330-room hotel has secretarial facilities for visiting businessmen, a shopping arcade, swimming pool, sauna and tennis-courts. It has a conference room for 1,000 people which can also be used for occasions like the annual Caledonian Society Ball, an amazing mix of kilts and *dishdashas*.

Expatriates like Dubai because of its attractive location, excellent shopping and bright social life, but, as in Bahrain and Qatar are obliged to live in hotels because of the accommodation shortage. Residential building in Dubai cannot keep pace with the demand, with the crisis likely to last another three years. No matter what one is prepared to pay, there is no accommodation; a three-bedroom villa in Deira costs DH75,000, which rises to DH100,000 in Jumeira, payable one year in advance.

Of course these high rents in the Gulf are partially self-inflicted as a result of oil price increases. As overheads rise in the West, so the buck is passed to the East; it costs an expatriate family of four £100 a week in rent to live in Dubai.

Concerned at the effect of inflation on the poor, Sheikh Rashid has ordered the construction of 3,000 low-cost homes and a DH200 million fund for developing property at a low, 1 per cent interest rate. Free land, with water and fencing, is offered to farmers in the irrigated Ruwaye Valley area. He also gave land to settle the poor migrant workers in a sort of *barasti* ghetto, outside Deira. This was a

Dubai Inter-Continental.

الإنتركونتنتال في دبي .

clever move, to get them off the streets — to keep Deira clean, as someone put it.

Social Change

While it was the initial appeal of Dubai which inspired this book, it has changed in the short time it has taken me to write it; from being the most romantic city, Dubai has changed into the 'big, bad place on the Gulf'.

In *Arabian Sands*, Thesiger concludes that 'the Arabs are a race which produces its best only under conditions of extreme hardship and deteriorates progressively as living conditions become easier'.

One actually sees this happening in Bahrain and Dubai, particularly in relation to alcohol. It is strange that some races cannot tolerate drink, and the Arabs are one; there are already 22,000 confirmed alcoholics in the Gulf, mainly in these two sheikhdoms. Even educated Arabs do not know how to drink; I had dinner with one gentleman who ordered bacon and eggs with Cognac.

When I stayed in Dubai in 1974, one was treated with traditional courtesy, but following several experiences there, all relating to officials who were supposed to look after me, I would be uneasy now.

The influx of prostitutes in Dubai is another factor making life difficult for a Western woman staying in an hotel, as the hotels are used for soliciting.

The Englishwoman who runs the 'call-girl' racket visits Dubai regularly with her catalogue from which locals pick their fancy. The cost is £200 a week, plus the return air fare and one or two gold watches thrown in. When the week is up, the girls go free-lance.

The new oil wealth and subsequent Westernisation of Dubai has seen other changes for the worse. Only two or three years ago, one could stroll along its creek in perfect safety. To me, this was the most charming place in the Gulf, the great *boums* at anchor with their crews brewing coffee and all traditional smells and sounds of the East.

Now one risks a mugging, and even in daylight an Indian tried to snatch my handbag. This is the price of wealth and Westernisation — alcoholism, prostitution, robberies and road accidents.

Dubai's Sheikh Rashid Hospital, owned by Sheikh Rashid, is one of the best in the Gulf with the most modern cardiac-monitoring equipment and the latest photo-therapy techniques for treating jaundice. It is staffed by 500 state-enrolled nurses who are predominently Indian, and the matron is Miss Holloway, who speaks fluent Arabic after 26 years experience in the Middle East.

'The day is not far away when we will do open-heart surgery in Dubai,' she predicted.

This was a contrast to her following remark about an affliction which is known as 'salt scarring', something which the matron had never encountered in her years in the Middle East.

'Shortly after they deliver, many women from the interior of Dubai, and also from Ras al-Khaimah and Fujairah, pack their vaginas with raw sea salt. The subsequent scarring causes their vaginas to constrict, thereby giving greater pleasure to their husbands, but the result is excruciatingly painful for the woman and it can cause both her and the unborn baby's death, as the neck of the cervix becomes so constricted that a Caesarean is the only means of delivery; A Bedouin woman in her desert *barasti* will die if she does not go immediately to hospital when labour begins.'

Adult admissions at the Rashid are usually suffering the normal maladies of any country in the Middle East, and like all Gulf hospitals, it receives many road-accident cases.

'Every day we receive some appalling road-accident victim,' concluded Matron Holloway. 'One morning I arrived on duty to find six dead and twenty-one injured, from a collision on the Sharjah Road.' And the speed at which the taxi bore me back to my hotel made me fearful of being her newest casualty.

A good road network links Dubai to the other emirates. At European speed, Abu Dhabi is two hours drive and it takes about an hour to travel to Ras al Khaimah. The adjacent sheikhdom of Sharjah is a ten to forty minute drive across the desert, depending on the traffic-jam.

SHARJAH

When I first stayed in Dubai, little interest was shown in its neighbour Sharjah, only five miles down the road, but when I returned a year later, in 1975, I was astonished at the development.

With oil on-stream, Sharjah had sprung to life with a tremendous vigour; foundations that I had photographed on the Sharjah Road were having their roofs hammered on and an 'Acapulco' was rising beside the once solitary Sharjah Carlton Hotel.

The pace at which all projects proceed in the Emirates is personified by Sharjah, ruled by H.H. Sheikh Sultan bin Mohammed al-Qasimi, who assumed power following his brother's murder in 1972. A graduate in agriculture from the University of Cairo, Sheikh

Sheikh Sultan, Ruler of Sharjah, with the author.

المؤلفة مع الشيخ سلطان . حاكم الشارقة .

Sultan is the UAE's most educated ruler, a gracious man of 38 who speaks English, Urdu, Farsi and French, as well as his native Arabic.

Despite the British presence, when Sharjah was used as an air base, few improvements were made to upgrade local living standards and therefore, like Abu Dhabi, it had to start from scratch.

'When we discovered oil, we devised a five-year plan to develop Sharjah, but we have worked so hard, it has almost been accomplished in three years,' Sheikh Sultan told me. 'It embraces all aspects of infrastructure, commerce, agriculture, sport, culture and tourism — anything to benefit the people,' he continued.

Together with his economic adviser, a shrewd clean-cut American called Bart Paff, the sheikh has devised some of the Gulf's most flamboyant schemes to wrest his country from the desert.

'Smile, you're in Sharjah' says a sign as one crosses the Dubai border, and while there is still little to smile about, if the sheikh's dreams materialise, Sharjah could become the most agreeable place to live in the Gulf.

Development

'Try to imagine a site for your Middle East operations that has a free enterprise economy, a strong currency, minimal governmental regulations, no foreign exchange controls and only nominal tariffs... Imagine that it is an international transport and communications centre with unlimited land for development...and that this place has no income tax, no sales tax, no property tax, no valued added tax, no capital gains tax, no estate tax...low labour costs and no unions. And imagine that this multinational business centre would really welcome your firm...There is such a place. It's the Emirate of Sharjah,' extolled an advertisement in the 10 December 1976 *Financial Times* supplement exclusively on Sharjah.

Given the fact it is somewhat jumping the gun, to a prospective investor it sounds like a paradise. While all the Emirates encourage foreign investment, none lays out the welcome mat like Sharjah. Bert Paff explained that the sheikh himself is the reason why people go there, largely because he favours the private sector and discourages the use of middlemen. 'Our basic approach is we don't have rules,' he told me. 'The sheikh is also anxious to avoid the large and inefficient bureaucracy which has been developed by Arab expatriates elsewhere. He believes in giving businessmen their freedom, thus the business environment is better here. Businessmen feel more comfortable, a local partner is not necessary and there is no reversionary rule governing property which makes for higher standards in construction.'

Sharjah has already attracted many prestigious industrial concerns as their regional headquarters, among them Dunhill, British Reinforced Concrete, Honeywell, Hempel Paints, ETPM the French oil industry supplier, Westinghouse, Armco Steel, 3M Corporation, Renault and Archirodon, the Greek company handling the port developments.

Until sandstorms silted up Sharjah's creek in the fifties, it was an entrepôt of almost equal importance to Dubai, but when this occurred, many merchants transferred their business down the road and Sharjah began to decline, a slide from which it is now recovering with a vengeance.

A £25 million project has dredged the creek and seven of twenty berths are complete at Port Khalid. However, Sharjah is not merely involved in port extensions, but is designing the first intermodular freight system in the Gulf with container terminals in Port Khalid, Khor Fakkan and the new Sharjah Airport.

'Roll on/roll off' is the answer to congestion in Gulf ports and the success of the initial berths in Sharjah has now prompted Dubai to build its own. And although Port Khalid is small compared to its giant competitor, its different policy may see some shift in trade away from Dubai where on any day, more than fifty ships lie 'on the the roads'.

'Port Rashid is just a giant warehouse with over a million tons of cargo left there as the cheapest place to store it. In order to promote the rapid transit of goods, Sharjah will charge ten times the storage fees of Dubai,' explained Bart Paff.

What may revolutionise the flow of freight to Gulf destinations is the container port under construction at Khor Fakkan, 55½ miles from Sharjah, on the Gulf of Oman. Until recently a sleepy fishing community, it is now being transformed into an in-transit port, able to take the world's largest container ships, carrying up to 1000 40-foot containers.

Dredging is unnecessary as the water is naturally deep and there are many advantages for ships to discharge in Khor Fakkan. Primarily it is the saving of £40,000-£45,000 in not having the extra sailing time around to Port Khalid. One ship is estimated to pass through the Straits of Hormuz every 12 minutes, and if this increases, it may become necessary to buy a ticket to enter the Gulf, as with Suez, not to mention the congestion of ships and drilling platforms, once inside.

Sharjah is therefore turning its natural geographic assets into commercial advantages. Located in the middle of the Emirates, it is seen as a central distribution point and the two ports, trucking system and airport, known as 'Sharjahport', will enable goods to be rapidly shifted by any route.

In the early thirties, Sharjah had the first airport of importance in the Gulf when it was a staging-post for Imperial Airways (forerunner to BOAC) on its Asian routes. This was seen to be obsolete and a new category II airport was opened in January 1977.

Many people see this airport as an unnecessary extravagance in Sharjah's search for status, plus further sand-slinging at Dubai. On an initial glance this seems correct, since the airport is situated 10½ miles from Sharjah, while Dubai's excellent terminal is only 15 minutes' drive, both close enough to come under the same traffic control. In fact Dubai's airport is no longer able to cope with the vast quantities of freight, but since Sharjah has announced its intention of offering a specialised cargo airport, Sheikh Rashid has declared he will turn Dubai's existing airport over to freight and build a new passenger-handling terminal at Jebel Ali.

Sharjah Airport is the first fully containerised terminal in the Middle East, and it also allows airlines to handle their own cargo.

The airport authority estimates that 35 per cent of traffic will arrive by sea and Paff anticipates goods will become airborne within two hours of being unloaded in Khor Fakkan, something inconceivable in either England or Australia.

Designed by Halcrow, the airport resembles a group of low-slung mosques. An airport hotel is under construction, also an American-style 'Industrial Park' complex to enable businessmen to virtually walk off a plane into their office. Flyovers will be erected over feeder roads to avoid congestion. The original airport has been scrapped, leaving new visitors perplexed as to why the once adjacent mosque is named 'Masjid al-Matar', or 'Airport Mosque'.

Sharjah currently resembles one huge construction site and, unless one sees the town plans, building appears as reckless as in Abu Dhabi. In truth, urban development in Sharjah is far superior to other places with the town divided into distinct commercial, financial, educational and industrial zones, interspersed with 'green belt'.

Sheikh Sultan takes a personal interest in town planning. Realising it is impossible for everyone to have a garden, he is building many small, high-walled public gardens into which a family can drive and picnic in total privacy. The palms struggling to survive along the Sharjah Road come from his private plantation.

A symbol of westernisation.

Whereas market produce used to be sold from fly-blown stalls along the creek, today a spectacularly designed central *souq* is being built, reflecting the sheikh's philosophic attitude in preserving, as far as possible, the traditions of his people.

'We are building it in one place, to gather the people together so they may exchange news, as they shop, like they used to do when they rode on camels to the old bazaars,' he told me. The 600-shop *souq* consists of four domed buildings supported by Moorish style columns. It features colourful mosaic tilting in a real attempt to introduce romance into Gulf architecture, the creation of White, Young and Partners of London.

In the UAE, where outdoor activity is limited by the torrid climate, cultural centres are seen as essential in the absence of a mixed social life, also to nurture the craving for knowledge and entertainment denied until the flow of oil wealth. Sharjah is building a big cultural centre containing a theatre, a library and hobby rooms which will act as a nucleus for smaller centres located in outlying villages. Women have a separate centre, almost 2 miles distant at Halwan; then there are sports stadiums, the Shaap Club and Sharjah International Club especially for expatriates.

Sabkha off Sharjah has been dredged to create lagoons and islands, on one of which is built a sort of Arabian Battersea Park with a zoo, aquarium, museum and merry-go-rounds. It is reached via the new bridge from the financial district on Boorj Avenue.

Sharjah probably boasts more banks *per capita* than anywhere else in the world; 31 were licensed in December 1976, but the older established British banks still enjoy the bulk of business. Sharjah's ambitions in the banking sphere are no less grandiose than its communications projects. In Boorj Avenue, already dubbed Sharjah's 'Wall Street', it plans to create a completely self-sufficient financial centre. Twenty-four eleven-storey blocks are being built along the boulevard, financed by the banks which will occupy the street level. The remainder is for shops, restaurants and residences, with each block linked by pedestrian bridges.

Associated with the project is the 22-storey 'Twin Tower' to house financial, but non-banking institutions, such as the Currency Board, insurance agents, accountants and the Sharjah Stock Exchange. Stock exchanges are still in their infancy in the Lower Gulf and cannot be seen as serious by Western standards. It is still too easy for locals to reap big profits from real estate and as 'sleeping partners' in Western investments for them to be interested. The government hopes to rectify this by creating public companies such as the trucking section of 'Sharjahport'.

Government House is the sheikh's splurge, a vast white-domed edifice resembling the sort of railway station the British might have built in India. It contains his *majlis* and the offices of his secretary, adviser and other officials. Lost in its vast marble entrance hall, I met one of the interior decorators clutching a pile of curtains.

'Now it is finally finished', he said, 'they want to take all the windows out and make them vertical!'

An even bigger monument in the vast de Gaulle Centre, a far-fetched scheme to house 15,000 people wholly within its confines.

'There will be no need to leave', said Paff, 'you can spend your whole life inside.'

The Fellini-style city within a town is the brainchild of the Arabian Development Real Estate Company, comprising Kuwaiti, Lebanese and local investors and the Renault Overseas Development Corporation — hence the salute to de Gaulle.

Building has been delayed because Dubai claimed the site on the outskirts of Sharjah. Neither can it please Sheikh Rashid that its five forty-storey blocks will be taller than his Trade Centre, but it is only a matter of time before it too is surpassed.

The Pakistani Deputy Chief Engineer of Sharjah Municipality estimates 40 international companies are involved in developing Sharjah. He also says a good company can erect a ten-storey building in ten months which must be the fastest rate in the world.

As well as the 50 high-rise buildings rising along Sharjah Road, a strip of desert when I drove it in 1974, are the many low-cost houses being built by federal, local and private investment. It is impossible to look in any direction in Sharjah without seeing an office-block, an hotel or a school under construction.

Education

Sharjah pioneered education in the former Trucial States with the establishment of the first school in 1953. Other educational distinctions are the first trade school in the UAE, which opened in 1958, and also the first school for girls. The University of Maryland has now opened a branch in the Emirate with courses in business management and commerce which can be accredited on the American system. A sign 'University of Maryland' stands at ankle height in the sand.

One of the major concerns of a European in the UAE used to be where to educate his children, for in the past, a posting there meant long separations while they attended home-country boarding schools. Aware that a harmonious social environment will attract foreign businessmen, Sheikh Sultan is making great efforts in the direction of education, certainly for his own people, but also for expatriate children. There are now six specialised schools in Sharjah, the most prestigious of which is the National College of Choueifat, which transferred from Lebanon during the civil war.

The college is an internationally accredited school whose standards are acceptable at all British universities and most American ones. Pupils are taken from the age of 3½-18 years and current attendance sees children of thirty different nationalities. Choueifat College is the most sought-after school in the Gulf and plans intend enlarging its three campuses to accommodate 3,000 students. A feature in Sharjah's urban planning is that all its schools are located in 'green belt' zones, although it will take as long for the trees to grow as for the children to graduate.

Agriculture

When one considers that the sheikh has a degree in agriculture, it is surprising that greater progress has not been made in farming, but Sharjah faces the same problem as elsewhere in that the Bedouin are not interested.

'We are trying to teach them farming methods, but transition is slow, despite the incentive of interest-free loans,' he explained.

The traditional agricultural area in Sharjah is on the coast near Khor Fakkan, but production here is limited to the narrow strip between the mountains and the sea where dates and citrus fruits are grown.

Ghrharaif, which lies inland, near the date oasis of al-Dhayd, has a good water table of some 60 feet. It is hoped to teach its Bedouin inhabitants farming, dairying, cattle-raising and poultry-farming.

'We have built thirteen new resettlement areas for them, but we are not insisting they move in from their oases as the change will occur gradually as their children are educated,' explained Sheikh Sultan.

Tourism

The whole of Sharjah is in a state of change, but of all projects in the place British airmen once called 'hell on earth' none is more amazing than hotel construction. From having only 250 rooms divided between three hotels in 1975, by 1978 Sharjah will boast 3,600 rooms in 35 hotels and motels.

Since Abu Dhabi is now recognised as being the political nucleus of the UAE and Dubai its commercial centre, Sharjah's aim is to become its leading tourist resort which is interesting from the psychological aspect since this is the ultimate process of Westernisation.

Many people feel Sharjah has over-reacted to the hotel accommodation crisis, but if the number of business visitors continues and domestic tourism develops, hotels should have no occupancy problems.

The initial idea is to create facilities for local tourists, but Sheikh Sultan believes his country's salubrious winter climate will lure Europeans. For the Gulf Arabs, Sharjah is ideal for brief festive periods and it is likely to replace Bahrain, which offers nothing like the same accommodation.

The unfortunate impact of tourism is that Khor Fakkan, one of the most beautiful parts of the Gulf, is being spoiled by developers. The coastline here has always been a favourite of Gulf expatriates who camp along the beaches like tribes of nautical Bedouin. The rocky inlets remind one of an unspoilt Riviera, washed by the same azure-coloured sea with calm bays for water-ski-ing. Hotels and villas are now under construction, but the biggest development is in central Sharjah, where an hotel, or motel, will open every month for the next two years.

On Khan Beach the sheikh has staked out the best position for himself where the Professional Group of Australia has built him a luxurious villa complex dubbed 'Garden City'. Sharjah's most prestigious new hotel is the 350 room Inter-Continental being built at the creek mouth and its most imaginative project is the Spanish Beach Club, owned by and modelled on the famous Marbella Club.

The good aspect of the advent of so many hotels is the healthy competition it will create, No longer will a third-grade hotel such as the Sheba be able to charge exorbitant rates, and the peeling Carlton Sharjah will be forced to have a face-lift. Competition for clients should see a high standard develop in the hotel industry in Sharjah. In this it can act as pace-setter for the rest of the Gulf states, which charge some of the world's highest rates for substandard food and service. It is likely that an hotel school will be established, as suggested in the three-year tourism development study.

To emphasise its seriousness about tourism, Sharjah commissioned Lufthansa to assess its potential attractions. These are seen to be the urban area of Sharjah, the coastal towns of Khor Fakkan and Dibba, and the oasis al-Dhayd where 50-100 great vehicles are smashing a new four-lane highway through the desert.

'We will develop Al-Dhayd in the same way as Williamsburg, Virginia,' said ideas man Paff. 'It will be along the lines of a luxurious tent village, highlighting the Arab heritage, with such attractions as camel races.'

The high air fares to the Gulf and the exorbitant cost of living are

major obstacles in Lufthansa luring tourists to Sharjah, but the biggest obstacle seems to be one that no one has considered, in that the federal UAE government does not grant tourist visas.

If Sharjah's modern landmark is Government House, its most familiar sight is the old Rola tree which once stood outside the town and is now surrounded by it. Believed to be more than 200 years old, it used to be the scene of traditional twice-yearly celebrations when marriages were arranged under its gnarled and twisted limbs.

Oil

The making of modern Sharjah began in 1969 when oil was discovered near the island of Abu Musa, 34 miles offshore. Work temporarily ceased when the barren island was claimed by Iran, when the British withdrew in 1971, but with oil known to exist in the vicinity, the American concession company Buttes formed Crescent Petroleum. Drilling recommenced in 1972 and commercial production began in July 1974. It now runs at around 50,000 barrels daily which places Sharjah even below Bahrain in the Gulf state oil producers, although the prospects of onshore oil are considered good.

Revenues are not commensurate with production, since Sharjah is obliged to pay the Shah 50 per cent, and because of a past dispute over borders, 30 per cent of its remaining share to Umm al Qaiwain. In May 1976, the *Financial Times* estimated Sharjah's petroleum revenues around £20-23 million.

AJMAN

The smallest Emirate in the UAE and the tiniest sheikhdom on the Gulf, Ajman is tucked into Sharjah like a pocket-handkerchief. The fact that a state of only 100 square miles could survive at all, is attributable to the 'Trucial System'.

It consists of the township of Ajman which is built on a ribbon-like creek, three miles north of Sharjah, and two inland enclaves in the mountains near Muscat, the date oases of Manama and Masfut.

Ajman's population of 21,566 is engaged in the sea-trades of fishing, weaving fish-traps and boat-building. Its boat-building industry is the biggest in the UAE, and all construction is done by hand.

Riggers working off Sharjah.

عمال النفط في الشارقة .

Fishing and boat-building in Ajman.   صيد السمك وبناء السفن حرف قديمة في عجمان.

As a non-oil-producer, Ajman has a positive attitude to the union and its ruler, H.H. Sheikh Rashid bin Humaid al-Nuaimi, is one of its most delightful personalities. Over six feet tall, he sports a splendid white beard, a true Arabian-style Father Christmas.

Federal government aid has deepened Ajman's port where a 'mini' dry dock is being built by a Japanese consortium including Mitsui and Nippon Steel. When complete, it will repair boats up to 8,000 tons; the first stage of the project cost £6 million and it is expected to be completed by 1978.

Federal aid has also paid for the cost of Ajman's sewage works and has built nine schools, including a 100-pupil boarding school at Masfut. It has also extended the hospital and constructed twenty miles of roads.

Two hundred low-cost homes have been built and there is a boom in private investment in the housing industry. Some nice villas have been built along the beach and Ajman's comparatively stable rents are attracting many expatriates working in Sharjah and Dubai.

For years, the biggest edifice in Ajman was a montrous lime-green cinema on the town perimeter. Today the town itself is developing slowly, and it has its own bank — the Ajman Drive-In Bank, the first one in the Emirates.

The interesting aspect about this tiny state is that it has developed some of the most unusual, non-oil-associated projects in the Gulf.

A spring bubbling at the head of the *Wadi Gulfa*, near Masfut, long a favourite picnic spot of local sheikhs, was discovered to be rich in minerals. In collaboration with Evian of France, a DH20 million mineral-water factory has been built there, bottling 18 million annually. I drank 'Gulfa' throughout my visit to the UAE; it resembles 'Evian' and undersells imported brands by as much as 50 per cent.

Marble deposits of 37 different shades are also found in Masfut, of such quality that even the connoisseurs of Carrera are impressed. The Lebanese-backed Ajman Marble factory was founded in 1970, although supplies barely meet local demand. Many of the sheikhs are fond of marble for their palaces: the Ruler's Son, Sheikh Humayd, has a home built largely of Masfut marble, and it also appears throughout Government House in Sharjah.

An oil refinery with a projected capacity of 200,000 barrels daily is currently under discussion by the Emirates, and in anticipation, Ajman has already planned an industrial zone.

With or without the refinery, it is seen that the Emirate is making a valiant effort to be self-supporting, although it obviously could not survive without the union.

Apart from the traditional boat-building, it has little to interest the casual visitor and new construction in the centre of town has blocked out its old fort which was anyhow an odd conglomeration of Portuguese-type bastions and Persian wind-towers, superimposed on a sort of ancient Abu Dhabi Hilton.

UMM AL QAIWAIN

The Emirate of Umm al Qaiwain lies three miles north of Ajman. It is cut off from the mainland by shimmering lagoons, a favourite wading-spot of sea-birds. Beyond a surf sweep long, white beaches where groups of camels stand staring out to sea.

The drive into Umm al Qaiwain affords a charming view of this somnolent little town of coconut-ice-coloured houses stacked around the bay.

Its biggest building is a fine seventeenth-century fort which the British bombarded in 1820, when Umm al Qaiwain sustained itself on fishing, pearling and the odd shipment of slaves. Today it is the police headquarters.

Umm al Qaiwain is still very much an 'Old Gulf Coast' town, as yet bypassed by development. Along its harbour, fishermen repair nets in the shade of their *sambuqs;* one I noticed had eyes like pearls, but his gnarled fingers moved deftly over the seine, twisting and looping more swiftly than the others.

Most of Umm al Qaiwain's population of 16,879 still live at subsistence level with fishing their main livelihood.

The Emirate's best short-term prospects lie in upgrading fishing from an individual basis into a commercial viability. Federal aid has deepened the creek and built a small cargo port and the Norwegian company Norconsult has designed a fish-oil factory to produce 300 tons a day.

Delicious fresh seafood is served at the Casino Umm al Qaiwain, which is recommended for lunch if one is driving up to Ras al Khaimah. To date the Emirate's only restaurant, it is not a casino but a pleasant beach cafe, patronised by local families on Fridays.

When I had lunch there, a strange gentleman approached and said that the Crown Prince would like an hotel for Umm al Qaiwain. If I knew of anyone, he said, the prince would provide the land, the company could take all the revenue for the first five years, after which it would revert to a managerial basis.

Since then, two hotels have been planned for the Emirate, one in *Falaj al-Mu'alla,* a rather improbable site in a saucer-sized inland oasis.

At Jabr Oasis, a start in agriculture has been made with Somali cattle and, all being well, it is hoped the farm will support some 5,000 beasts, but the region is so hot in summer that the cattle only drink during the day, feeding in the relative cool of night. Australian 'siritro' grass is being cultivated and the Emirates Livestock Company and Abu Dhabi Development Bank have financed a chilled meat store.

Sixteen per cent of the people are engaged in agriculture but because there is no real commercial activity to date, there is no actual merchant class.

Offshore oil exploration continues and in anticipation of a 'strike', the Municipality of Umm al Qaiwain is planning for an expected population increase of 50,000 in the next five years! *Inshallah,* there is nothing like hope! As in the other Gulf State 'have-nots', people see no logical reason why oil, which has been discovered all along the Eastern Arabian littoral, should suddenly stop in Sharjah.

Blind fisherman in Umm al Qaiwain.

صيادوا السمك في عجمان .

Meanwhile, the federal budget provides schools, roads, clinics, electricity and the building of low-cost houses. Before this construction, ruler H.H. Sheikh Ahmed bin Rashid al-Moalla's palace stood alone on a stretch of isolated beach, a long red Cadillac parked outside. Today it overlooks a sea of flat-topped houses and the main road has modern street lights. When I first visited Umm al Qaiwain in 1974, wooden sticks doubled as street-lamps and telephone poles. Change is coming, albeit slowly.

RAS AL-KHAIMAH

Any remark by a local pertaining to development in Ras al-Khaimah terminates with a confident 'when we have our oil'. Not 'if we discover oil' or 'should we discover oil', but a very positive 'when'.

In June 1976, Maurice Jadaa, manager of Vitol Exploration, the Dutch consortium drilling 31 miles offshore, told me seismic results were very encouraging. Geared for a major find, it therefore came as a shock when Vitol discovered only enough oil to produce about 4,000 barrels of good crude a day and the company now needs to find substantially more to make its operations viable. Two more wells are being drilled and the results are expected to become known in late 1977.

In its aspiration of becoming a rich oil producer, Ras al-Khaimah shares the common dream of Ajman, Umm al-Qaiwain and Fujairah, but otherwise it is quite different to the Emirates of the Lower Gulf.

Geographically it resembles northern Oman, from which it is divided by the jagged Hajar Range of mountains which attract some 200 mm of rain a year. Equally blessed with springs and a relatively fertile soil, Ras al-Khaimah is by nature an agricultural state and both its history and its contemporary outlook reflect its individuality. It also has Arabia's only casino. The casino is another Gulf anomaly, since betting is forbidden by the Koran, but although Ras al-Khaimah's censors ink bras on to bare-topped girls in the *News Of The World,* gambling is allowed, although UAE nationals are not supposed to play.

After losing at roulette in the casino, I decided to stay and watch as two sloppily dressed men slipped on to the stools beside me. The Lebanese manager whispered that they were the Galadari brothers from Dubai, the Iranian merchant family which owns, among many investments, the Dubai State Bank, the Inter-Continental Hotel franchise and the new Galadari Cementation Construction Limited, and who are reputed to be as wealthy as the Ruler himself.

The younger man watched as his brother scattered the pink and black DH500 chips about the board like seeds. But I realised that he had lost, as a croupier passed him a DH40,000 chit to sign. 'His credit is good,' someone said, and play began again.

Ras al-Khaimah is named after the custom practised by the great-grandfather of its present ruler, H.H. Sheikh Saqr bin Muhammed al-Qasimi, who used to keep a torch burning above his tent to guide night caravans to his hospitality.

In 1747, the al-Qasimi tribe established itself in this region at the mouth of the Gulf, its great dhows controlling the Straits of Hormuz, repelling repeated invasions by the colonial powers.

It is said the fleet numbered more than 800, with a crew of 20,000, and it was not until 1820 that British forces destroyed the fleet, which was threatening its trade with India and, along with the other states, the once great Gulf sea power signed the 'Treaty of Peace in Perpetuity'.

When the Union of Arab Emirates was formed in 1971, Sheikh Saqr held off joining for what are generally considered to be two reasons: Ras al-Khaimah's history of fierce independence and a hope that the discovery of oil might enable it to pursue an independent course, like Bahrain and Qatar. Today the sheikh still waits for the miracle and it is still felt that Ras al-Khaimah might secede, if large quantities of oil are ever found.

There is no overt reason for this, although some of its projects, primarily the airport and earth station, display a notorious individuality.

Both projects were financed by Saudi Arabia. In an interview with the *Gulf Mirror* in December 1975, the Sheikh said: 'They [the Saudis] look upon us with a special eye, the eye of a good mother.'

This is fortunate for Ras al-Khaimah, but it is a pity the aid is not used to intensify agricultural development, or in light industrial projects. Sheikh Saqr defends his £4 million International Airport as being necessary to facilitate industrial growth, farming and tourism, and as a convenient change-over point for tanker crews, but as of January 1977, still the only airline to fly there was a weekly service by Kuwait Air.

Gulf Air manager Salim bin Nassir al-bu Said said the airline had no immediate plans to extend when I spoke to him in June 1976, but since then, Sheikh Saqr himself has visited Bahrain to argue that as a member-owner of Gulf Air, the airline should have at least one flight there.

Seen honestly, both airport and earth station are the Emirate's search for status, and Sir William Halcrow, who also designed the new airport in Sharjah, must wonder where it all will end, since now even sleepy Fujairah wants an airport. The £5 million earth station is a genuine irritation to the other UAE rulers, as well it may be when the federal budget pays all Ras al-Khaimah's education, health and housing expenses. However, in Ras al-Khaimah it is claimed that being on Dubai territory, that Dubai operators give preference to Dubai calls.

Ras al-Khaimah has the most spectacular terrain in the Gulf. Mountains suddenly appear as one drives along the road from Umm al-Qaiwain; painted mauve against a washed-out sky, they come as a shock after the seemingly interminable flatness of the Upper Gulf.

The customary roundabout at the entrance to the Emirate offers a choice north, to Khor Khuwair, the future industrial zone, inland to the agricultural plain, or to the coastal capital of Rams.

Turning left takes one to Rams, a sleepy creekside town whose only concession to Westernisation is a forest of television aerials.

Its shops are typically Indian sub-continent, spilling velvet cushions, carpets, brassware and wicker-work. On the quay coal-black Arabs break lumps of salt and weigh it on ancient scales, *abras*

The *abra* ferry at Ras al-Khaima.   عبّارة في رأس الخيمة .

ferry passengers across to Gray McKenzie opposite, and further along is a fish market.

Twenty per cent of the population is employed in fishing, a speciality of which is the export of dried sharks' tails and fins to south-east Asia. The best season is September to March, when colder and less saline water flows into the Gulf from the Arabian Sea, bringing shoals of mackerel, sardines and tuna. Twelve miles north of Rams, a Norwegian company has built a fish-meal factory.

The UAE's fifth cement factory began production here in 1975. It has since changed from clay to silica rock, producing 250,000 tons of sulphur-resistant cement a year. Rock exports are another facet of the Emirate's non-oil-based economy; rock in Abu Dhabi's breakwater comes from Ras al-Khaimah which is also the main supplier for Saudi Arabia's new port at Jubeil. Kuwaiti investment is in a £7 million asbestos and sand-brick factory, but the biggest outside investment is in a nine-berth port being built by Mothercat and Archirodon.

The American company of MacDermott is rolling more than 6000 pipes a month for export in the Middle East but this is the extent of any manufacturing industry.

'In what fields would the government like to participate?' I asked of the plump, balding official in the Ministry of Information.

'We would like a steel factory, since His Highness does not expect the oil to last forever.'

'But your oil is not yet on-stream,' I replied, astonished.

'Yes, but it still won't last forever,' he repeated, disappearing behind his paper.

'What is the annual income from fishing in Ras al-Khaimah?' I tried again.

'Enough for food,' he briefly looked up from the news.

'What is the gross national income?' I asked, my temper rising.

'I don't know anything about the income,' he said. 'Nobody knows what the income is in Ras al-Khaimah and what is more, they have no budget. How can they, if they don't have an income?'

Feeling like Alice listening to the Red Queen, I excused myself and left. The manager of the Chamber of Commerce was of no value either, in fact everyone I met seemed to be living in a state of suspended expectation of discovering oil which would solve all their worries, including having to work.

The reality is that Ras al-Khaimah has the potential to one day supply the basic foodstuffs of the UAE. Turning right at the roundabout puts one on the road to the Digdagga Agricultural Station which was founded by an Englishman, Robin Huntingdon, in 1955.

His experiments pioneered Ras al-Khaimah's agriculture. There are now more than 500 farms of an average holding of five acres, and under the federal budget, farmers are supplied interest-free loans on equipment and fertilisers.

An estimated 18 per cent of Ras al-Khaimah's total 700 square miles is under cultivation with vegetables. Bananas, mangoes, strawberries, oranges, lemons, figs and paw-paws also grow with some tobacco in the inland enclave of Shamel al-Hawylat. Most crops are sold to Dubai, and the last guess at Ras al-Khaimah's income from agriculture was by its Ministry of Information which quotes it as QDR700,000 in the old currency, no doubt because someone like the lazy bureaucrat could not be bothered converting it into dirhams.

Digdagga Agricultural Station has 40 students who receive secondary education with emphasis on agriculture. Breeding experiments are conducted with English Friesians and the Ministry of Agriculture is paying for the installation of oxygen compounds to improve breeds. It is also constructing modern milking sheds.

Farther along from Digdagga is the hot-springs village of Khatt, which the government wants to develop as a spa resort. Khatt itself is a dusty, attractive settlement of narrow alleys running between high-walled houses, more like a town in central Oman than the UAE.

Its springs are deep, steaming, tourmaline-coloured pools fringed by date-palms. As I stood there, a Bedouin family was bathing, the mother complete with *burqa*, her *abaya* floating round her like an oil slick.

A spa resort in a cold climate seems more normal than one in the desert, but a German-type spa complex is planned at an estimated cost of DH100 million.

'When will construction begin?' I had asked of the bureaucrat. 'In two, three, maybe four years, when we get our oil,' he had replied.

Ras al-Khaimah would seem to have a future as a tourist resort. Although it endures the same hot, humid summers as the other Gulf States, its winters are more moderate and many sheikhs and merchants from as far afield as Kuwait own houses there. Inter-Continental will open a 250-room hotel in 1978; at present there is only one hotel, the Hotel-Casino Ras al-Khaimah.

The Emirate is also rich in archaeological remains, although most are in ruins because of neglect. It was the site of historic Julfar, an important port from ancient times to the early nineteenth-century and the distinctive cream and red Julfarware pottery is still picked up on many sites.

Every date plantation conceals a crumbling tower and the chain of forts topping the dunes beside the road from Umm al-Qaiwain dates from the original dynasty.

The small gap at the top of each fort was for dropping stones on invaders ascending by rope. Wind has scoured beneath some of the forts so that it seems, if one leaned on them, they might topple over.

So much remains to be discovered. Vague reports suggest that ruins north of Rams may be connected with the Kingdom of Sheba: *Qasr az-Zubba,* the 'Palace of the Queen of Zubba', or the Queen of Sheba? It is credible that the Queen of Sheba may have maintained a palace in ancient Ras al-Khaimah, a sort of 'frankincense connection' with the Yemen. Several frankincense routes are known to have existed and this may have been a distribution point for Lower Mesopotamia and the Indian sub-continent.

The authority on local history is Major Tim Ash, who was a former desert intelligence officer with the Trucial Oman Scouts and is now adviser to the Ras al-Khaimah Mobile Force of 600. He is also a friend of the Shihu, wild mountain tribesmen who lead a semi-autarkic existence, descending for the date harvest in Oman, then returning into their inhospitable environment where they live like troglodytes. One unusual aspect of their behaviour is the custom of uttering a series of short, sharp cries, like a dog barking, at mealtimes.

The Shihu are the last untamed tribe in Arabia and the government of the UAE leaves them alone. Only Major Ash visits their stronghold in the Hajar, firing his rifle in the foothills, like knocking on a door, to which they signal entry with a volley from above. Ash speaks their dialect and the short, tangle-haired men greatly respect him, always stopping for coffee at his house when they make one of their rare visits to Rams.

It will be a long time before a road is blasted into the Hajar, and staring up at its peaks, I wondered what life must be like for the women. As yet no Western woman has ever been up there and few men, save Major Ash.

Until 1971, the Gulf islands of the Tumbs belonged to Ras al-Khaimah, but only hours after the British withdrawal they were seized by Iran. Although there is now little he can do about it, Sheikh Saqr maintains they are incontestably part of his country. Despite the loss of the islands, Ras al-Khaimah still occupies a vital strategic position, since so much of the worlds' vital oil supplies passes through the narrow entrance between here and Iran.

FUJAIRAH

With the youngest ruler, 26-year-old H.H. Sheikh Hamed bin Mohammed al-Sharqi, Fujairah is also the poorest and least prestigious member of the UAE, although its population of 26,498 is more than the combined totals of Ajman and Umm al Qaiwain.

Until the road between Sharjah and Khor Fakkan was opened in 1975, one almost needed a magic carpet to reach Fujairah, the alternative being an 8-hour back-trip through the *wadis*. Today the journey takes 1¾ hours.

Entirely surrounded by Sharjah, the Emirate occupies 450 square miles on the Gulf of Oman, the Hajar Mountains rising straight off the coastal plain, which is never wider than a mile. Dates are grown and there is a small export trade in tobacco and dried limes, as on adjacent Batinah Coast in Oman.

The other occupation is fishing, although it is affected by the fringe of the summer monsoon from India. The usual boat is the simple palm-bound *shasha,* which is all the fishermen can afford.

H.H. Sheikh Hamad bin Mohammed al-Sharqi.

صاحب السمو الشيخ حمد بن محمد الشارقي .

Fisherman on the Fujairah beach.

صيادو السمك على الساحل في الفجيرة .

When I stood on the beach in Fujairah, three fishermen began hauling in their net and we all helped, heaving the rope as they crooned sea shanties. When it finally came ashore, the catch was a miserable six silver mullet, but we bought three from them and they disappeared, seemingly happy, to their palm *barastis*.

Driving into Fujairah, one passes a restored sand-buff fortress which the British also bombarded in 1825, in order to secure the release of Sheikh Hamad's slaves.

In *Farewell to Arabia,* David Holden relates how one day in 1850, Ronald Codrai, the newly appointed British political agent,

> ... having made his way over the mountains of the Musandam Peninsula to the village of Fujairah ... was set upon by the local sheikh, who demanded to know why he had shelled Fujairah 'yesterday' and destroyed the fort.
> Codrai, who had never seen the place before, requested an explanation in his turn, and discovered that — as so often happens in Arabia — the sheikh's measure of time was more poetic than precise. In fact he harbored a grudge from some 25 years earlier when ... the British had sent a sloop to lob a few admonitory shells into the village. Unfortunately, the captain had either omitted to put anyone ashore to explain his action, or had been unable to find the sheikh and his son...Codrai was the first Englishman to have set foot in the place since then...

Today a sand-scarred sign on what is presumably the border, announced that 'Fujairah Welcomes You', but one does not have this feeling as it is more like a dead town, or one whose inhabitants have fled before impending disaster, which could well be the twentieth-century. Only once did I see people in Fujairah, on UAE National Day, when Bedouin tribesmen performed a traditional dance outside Sheikh Hamad's palace. Hands clasped behind their backs, they shuffled up and down to a monotonous rhythm tapped on drums by a man who whirled like a dervish in their midst. One step forward and one step back, when they hit the ground with their camel sticks.

Fujairah's palace is the most unpalatial in the Gulf, devoid of any fountains or gardens, with a rough earth courtyard and empty 'Crown Cola' bottles stacked against the walls. It wears the air of a Hong Kong tenement, although were it Hong Kong, some 1,000 families would be living in it.

But if Fujairah is unknown in the outside world, then this is the strength of the UAE, for like Ajman and Umm al Qaiwain, it could not survive alone, or if it did, it would be classed as 'Fourth World',

Arab woman on the Batinah Coast of Oman. She wears the mask, or *burqa* and the black cloak, or *abaya*.

Wahda Ahmed Masoud, the first woman police officer in the Sultanate of Oman.

The market in Muscat with the *jabal* rising directly behind the town.

Bedouin men dancing outside the ruler's palace in Fujairah.

Omanis always look to the sea for a livelihood.

Al-Ruwais, northern Qatar.

Dannah or 'perfect pearl' worth £30,000.

Entrance to the Sultan's palace in Muscat, Oman.

from which it is anyhow not far removed.

The Abu Dhabi Town Planning Department has devised its first-ever town plan and the UAE Ministry of Public Works is financing a £30 million harbour with an initial three berths for ships to 15,000 tons and shelter for 100 fishing craft.

A £300,000 military camp at Murbah is financed by the UAE Ministry of Defence and more than 100 low-cost houses have been built in the villages of Qurayyan, Murbah, Lulluawayah and Dibba. Many are not yet occupied as the Fujairah people are rather more reluctant to change their ways of life and of course for the Shihu it is unthinkable.

Six schools have been built and a new hospital and post office. Until recently, Fujairah's only export income came from philatelic sales and, according to American academic John Duke Anthony, from selling bogus diplomatic passports!

Fujairah has the same ruggedly beautiful scenery as Khor Fakkan twelve miles north, and there seems no reason why it too cannot share in the potential UAE tourist industry. While there was not even a shop, or a bank, at the time of writing, construction was beginning on a 250-room Hilton!

Businessmen should note that the market in Fujairah is wide open, although there can be little local participation because of lack of funds. As the locals have been largely cut off from the effects of Westernisation on the Gulf proper, the promise of oil does not yet have the same significance as its does in Ajman, Umm al Qaiwain and Ras al-Khaimah, which are exposed to the wealth of Dubai and Abu Dhabi.

Reserve Oil and Gas of Denver is working the offshore concession, but the continental shelf is narrow, falling to unfathomable depths. Mineral surveys in the mountains are said to be encouraging, with reports of copper, chrome and even uranium. If not oil, then uranium is a worthy substitute on which, if it is found, Fuajairah can take a mighty jump into the seventies.

5 The Sultanate of Oman

The Sultanate of Oman occupies an area of 120,000 square miles on the southern littoral of Arabia. It includes a separate territory, the Musandam Peninsula, at the mouth of the Arabian Gulf. Common borders are with Saudi Arabia, the United Arab Emirates and the People's Democratic Republic of Yemen. The population of the Sultanate is estimated at 1.5 million, and the capital is Muscat, on the Gulf of Oman.

Ruler H.M. Sultan Qaboos bin Said replaced his father on 23 July 1970, pledging: 'I shall work with every possible haste to make your lives happier in preparation for a better future.'

'The big difference between Oman and the Gulf States is that undeniably the sudden changes are a shock for the Bedouin, but here we have our history for them to fall back on,' said Mr Khalfan Nasser al-Waheiby, Minister of Social Affairs and Labor in the Sultanate of Oman. 'As distinct from the newly rich Emirates, Oman has a cultural base,' he continued, as we spoke in the Ministry of Information building in Qurum, 7 miles from Muscat.

Four years ago the ministry was not there; five years ago, neither was Qurum, and barely a decade ago there was no development outside the walls of Muscat. At dusk, an old cannon was fired and its gates closed on the Sultan's Palace, the police headquarters and British Consulate, shutting out the only bank, taxis and other 'harbingers of the West' — by law of the absolute rule of Sultan Said bin Taimur bin Turki bin Faisal bin Said bin Sultan bin Ahmed bin Said al bu Said, the twentieth-century was kept at bay.

Sultan Said came to power in 1932, twelfth descendant of the al Bu Said dynasty, whose Imam was elected in 1749, but Oman's history stretches much further back into the skeins of time; it is

H.H. Sultan Qaboos bin Said.

صاحب الجلالة سلطان قابوس بن سعيد .

very long and very tangled, and because of the remoteness of the country, is hardly known.

Until now there have been few archaeological expeditions in Oman. Flint-stones indicate it was inhabited by primitive man and theories claim its beehive graves are linked with the ancient culture of Umm-an-Nar in Abu Dhabi. Burial cairns unearthed near Ibri date from 4 BC and fragments of Eastern pottery prove Oman had farflung commercial contacts some 6,000 years ago.

Situated on the shipping lanes between Africa and Asia, it was inevitable that Oman should develop into a great seafaring nation. An Omani, Abu Ubadya, sailed from Arabia to China 800 years before Columbus discovered America.

The seventh century saw the seatrade boom and boat-building keep pace. One of the earliest boats was the simple *shasha*, a canoe made of bundles of palms lashed together, through which the water freely flowed.

Another was the 10-15 feet long *houri*, whose planks were sewn with coconut fibre. Even up to the seventeenth century, all Omani boats were 'plank sewn'. The *shu'ais* and *boums* used for long voyages are still built in this traditional way at Sur, 130 miles south of Muscat.

In the tenth century, one of the most important ports was the old capital of Sohar, on the Batinah Coast, 120 miles north of Muscat. It is hard to imagine this today. An impoverished town of palm-roofed houses, it lies steeped in dreams of pristine glory on a long, grey beach, dotted with human faeces.

An interesting reminder of its past are the *shashas* still in use, although today polyfoam is packed under the palm-frond decks to give them added buoyancy. This is why one does not see the streets littered with the packing-cases of radios, tape-recorders and televisions that are pouring into Oman.

In 1507 when the Portuguese navigator Albuquerque the Great called at Sohar, it was a thriving town and its big, square fort was said to require a thousand men to defend it. Since then, the only other highlight occurred in 1866, when the seventh Sultan of the al bu-Said dynasty, while taking a siesta, was shot by his son.

When the Portuguese rounded the Cape in the sixteenth century, one of the first places they seized was Muscat, where they remained almost 150 years, until driven out. During the seventeenth century, Oman routed attacking Persians and conquered Portuguese strongholds in Mogadishu and Mombasa, also capturing the fabled 'clove isle' of Zanzibar. By the eighteenth century they had sent the Portuguese packing from East Africa, where Omani presence persisted another 250 years.

Ultimately Britain appeared. In 1798, fearing French designs on the Sultanate and India, it entered into the first of a series of 'friendship treaties' with Oman. After the death, in 1856, of the illustrious Sultan Said bin Sultan, Britain settled the subsequent dispute between his sons in the Canning Award which gave one son Oman and the other Zanzibar.

Largely because of the loss of its overseas territories, the advent of steam and the abolition of the slave trade, the Sultanate began a downhill slide, settling back to exist on fishing.

During the following years, the Sultan's authority was continually challenged by attacks from the interior and in 1895 Muscat was captured and the Sultan reinstated only with British help. In fact the British never dispossessed the Sultan and the country continued in medieval backwardness until the late 1960s.

Despite the discovery of oil in 1964, the isolation and poverty of Oman was not arrested until Sultan Qaboos came to power and while, like the Gulf States, its metamorphosis relates to oil, the still backward state of Oman is the result of nearly four decades of repressive rule by his father.

Although some writers have excused his attitude by saying he had a confirmed horror of becoming financially indebted to Britain, without doubt Sultan Said was, as David Holden describes him, 'the Scrooge of Arabia'. He shared this common meanness with Sheikh Shakhbut of Abu Dhabi, and even when Oman began earning from oil he still refused to spend anything on social welfare or economic development.

All Western influence was forbidden: schools, hospitals, radios, cars, bicycles — even sunglasses and cigarettes! The Sultan once sent a messenger across to the British Consul in Muscat to say he had seen him smoking on the balcony.

Muscat has the most fiendish climate in the world. The first four British Consuls died there, although it is not known whether from sunstroke or malaria. Today one must still take anti-malarial precautions, especially in the southern province of Dhofar.

Leastways if Muscat is changing, its climate is not. The wall of rock behind the town radiates such heat, it sears the eyeballs with temperatures of 120°F recorded at midnight!

Obviously outdoor labour is impossible under such conditions and, like the Gulf States, Oman slows down in summer, working only 7 a.m. − 1 p.m.

But slowing down is only relative and statistics best summarise the speed of development under Sultan Qaboos:

Gross National Product:	1970	£148 million
	1976-7	£970 million
Education:	1970	6,941 students
	1976	55,752 students
Hospitals:	1970	nil
	1976	15
Roads:	1970	7 miles
	1977	500 miles
Imports:	1970	£20 million
	1975	£812 million
Exports:	1970	£76 million
	1975	£393 million

This is the impact of oil and the endeavours of 37-year-old Sultan Qaboos who, after returning home from a Sandhurst education, was detained for six years by his father. In this the people recognise their own suffering and now that both are free, they openly display great affection for him.

Oil and Minerals

Oil exploration in the Sultanate of Oman is a continuing saga, in conditions more trying than most – the same furnace-like temperatures, but with added risk of attack from belligerent Bedouin.

The first company to explore was Petroleum Concessions Limited. An advance party making gravity surveys for drilling in 1962, on the fringe of the Empty Quarter, discovered two small fields, but missed the biggest deposits at Fahud.

Then in 1964 a major discovery was made at Fahud. Its three fields were linked and a pipeline laid 150 miles over the mountains to the terminal, *Mina al-Fahal,* near Muscat. The first shipment of crude oil was made on 1 August 1967.

Current plans envisage a 20,000 barrels per day refinery, to cost £5-8 million; at present all production is exported as crude.

In 1974, the government acquired a 60 per cent share of Petroleum Development Company of Oman (PDO), of which Shell had held 85 per cent and PARTEX 15 per cent. Oman does not belong to OPEC and by Gulf standards is not a big producer, pumping some 300,000 barrels a day. In 1975 oil revenues amounted to £859 million.

The main volume comes from the PDO concession areas at Fahud

A typical old Omani.

عماني عجوز

and south-east of there, the Ghaba Fields, which came on-stream in 1975. North-west of Fahud, near the UAE border, the Lekhwair Field started production in 1976 at 15,000 barrels per day.

Exploration continues with a generally optimistic view that more oil will be found. Wintershall is working concessions off the Batinah Coast, ELF-ERAP is drilling off the Musandam Peninsula and also on the edge of the Empty Quarter near the remote area of Butabul, in association with Sumitomo of Japan.

So much remains to be discovered in the Sultanate of Oman, whose rugged terrain and lack of communications are the main factors inhibiting faster exploration. The country is known to be rich in untapped mineral resources. Copper deposits are estimated at 18 million tons, and coal at 10 million tons. There is also evidence of chrome, manganese, asbestos and reputedly high-quality phosphate deposits in Dhofar.

In this, the Sultanate is fortunate since its future prosperity does not wholly depend on oil. Hence there is not the same rush towards industrial diversification, with current emphasis directed towards bolstering agriculture and fisheries.

Development

Discussions seem to take longer in Oman than the Gulf States. Final agreement on the 350,000-ton cement plant is elusive and plans for a large-scale gas liquefication plant have not yet matured, but it must be seen that Oman was fighting a civil war in Dhofar until 1975 and there is still massive spending on defence.

Industrial plans received a boost in October 1976 when the Arab, Kuwait and Abu Dhabi Funds agreed to a $100 million loan to finance the pipeline required to bring gas to the coast to fuel these projects, including the desalination plant, five miles north of Muscat. This £21 million joint Lebanese-German venture has an initial production capacity of 4 million gallons daily which can be increased to 6 million, one of the biggest in the Middle East.

The cost of water, like electricity, is exorbitant. To air-condition a three-bedroom house during the five summer months amounts to over £50 a month.

The inflation rampant throughout the Gulf reaches a peak in Oman, which is now the most expensive country in Arabia. The exorbitant price of drink staggers most businessmen; I paid £6 for a demi-carafe of Australian claret. A quick look at local market prices explains the cost of hotel food: tomatoes £1 a lb, a cauliflower £1.50, mince £2 a lb.

The first hotel built in Oman was the Al-Falaj, which opened in

1970. For some time it held the dubious honour of being listed in a *Time* magazine survey as the second most expensive hotel in the world. Happily, two more hotels have opened; the nearby Ruwi and the Gulf hotel on a cliff site, overlooking the sea. It is managed by John Thuillier, who is famous throughout Arabia for his enterprise — to celebrate National Day 1976, he imported ten members of the Dagenham Girl Pipers!

Everything is timed to open on National Day in Oman and in 1977 it hopefully will be the 300-room Inter-Continental.

Under Sultan Said there were no hotels, but then of course there were hardly any visitors. Even housing construction did not begin until late 1970 and the government's problem was so great that until 1973 it could only cope with the needs of its own employees by which time 7 ministries, 342 flats and 12 villas had been built.

One of the most visionary schemes is Qurum, where everyone in the media works and lives and seven miles up the coast is *Medinat Qaboos*, the Gulf's most spectacular housing project.

Dubbed the 'foreign quarter', the 18 million rial complex built by Taylor Woodrow and the International Development Company of Oman consists of 1,400 houses connected to a central commercial area, similar to Isa Town in Bahrain.

The most exciting feature is the architectural blend of old 'fort type' houses and modern living, but in Oman's climate, it is a strange blunder to have all the houses facing west.

As in the Gulf States, the cost of housing is huge. To rent a three-bedroom flat costs from £840 a month and one is unlikely to buy a house for less than £50,000.

Five miles from Muscat, Ruwi is Oman's first suburb, a mess of half-built office-blocks and cars churning across vacant allotments, coating anyone mad or brave enough to walk about in clouds of choking dust.

One evening I went out with a Belgian businessman who fell, with a Flemish yell, into one of Ruwi's enormous culverts. Lying on its edge, I could distinguish him dusting his suit on the bottom, and only with the aid of two Sikhs who knotted their turbans together did we manage to haul him out.

People who disapprove of such reckless building activity may take the comfort in fact that errors are often ruthlessly corrected. The Ruwi Cinema, only two years old, was bulldozed when it was realised that the new mosque would have too great a proximity!

Looking through the disorder, Ruwi would seem to have the makings of a model suburb. Its focal points will be a Civic Centre to contain the National Theatre and a Commercial Centre housing the

Chamber of Commerce, a Trade Centre and shops.

While capital expenditure on commerce and development amounted to £313 million in 1975, the Sultan is still criticised for extravagant spending on aesthetically pleasing things like fountains.

A late starter in the 'monuments race', Oman has exceeded even Sharjah in a spectacular fountain on the Ruwi roundabout, with the water illuminated by ever-changing rainbow-coloured lights. Indeed the way fountains are springing up in Muscat, it could become the 'Barcelona of Arabia'.

A terraced approach of fountains leads to the Sultan's palace on the waterfront in Muscat. Nowhere in the Gulf, nor for that matter in the entire Middle East, is there such an opulent building which retains all the pomp and pageantry of old Arabia. It is understood that Sultan Qaboos is in fact embarrassed by the vast blue, pink, white and gold tiled edifice, which is out of harmony with the simplicity of other Muscati architecture. So he keeps it for guests, remaining in his older palace at Sib.

According to Australian artist Ann Hill, who has visited his palaces in Sib and Salalah, they are little more than 'pleasant seaside residences'.

'They are really just nice homes and far less extravagantly furnished than the mansions of the UAE sheikhs,' she said. With her husband, sculptor Darryl, Ann lives in Oman, making films for the government.

A stark contrast to the palace is the Portuguese Fort Jalali, opposite Fort Merani where, in 1782, the Immam, Ahmed bin Said in Merani, and his sons Sultan and Seif in Jalali, bombarded each other across the bay.

Pending construction of a new prison, Fort Jalali is still Muscat's jail, its grim appearance matching its reputation as an Omani version of 'Devil's Island', where prisoners were either split on the rack, or grilled by the sun.

Before 1920, it was forbidden to leave Muscat since the Sultan's authority did not extend into the interior and one risked death from warring tribes, which is why geography books called the Sultanate 'Muscat and Oman'.

As a result of repression and isolation, Muscat went to sleep, and even today it is not fully aroused, for apart from the arm-waving policeman outside the *Bab al-Kabir,* or the 'Big Gate', life outside still moves at the pace of the past.

Enveloped in black *abayas,* the women walk in pairs, or fours, and commerce is conducted slowly, or not at all. By noon, the white buildings dazzle in the blinding sun and everyone withdraws indoors.

During the afternoon, nothing stirs, just starlings darting at flies. At dusk the *banyanis,* or Indian merchants, open their shops again and coffee-houses begin to fill with turbanned men. Outside Grindlays Bank, cars begin to queue up on the road to Muttrah, Muscat's twin city, two miles round the bay.

In 1970, there were only six miles of sealed roads in the whole of Oman. Today, nearly 500 miles have been laid, slowly, and with a great deal of sweat, opening up the interior. Naturally road construction has seen a vast increase in the number of vehicles registered, from 840 in 1970 to 20,000 in 1976, and, although the Omani is generally a better driver than the Gulf Arab, a subsequent fatality rate of nil to 155 (1974).

Even widening the Muscat-Muttrah roadway has done little to ease the traffic-jams. Abetting the problem is the absence of a public transport system as everyone travels by taxis which park, with one or two remaining donkeys, outside the vestige of Muttrah Gate.

Muttrah is much more lively and colourful than Muscat, and as someone aptly said, it seems to have a foot in Africa, the other in India and its trunk in Arabia itself. A superb corniche curls round a bay backed by elegant old Persian- and Indian-style houses of

Old houses in Muttrah.   بيوت جميلة على الشاطئ في المطرح .

several storeys, broken by blue and green window shutters. With Dubai's wind-towers, Muttrah shares the last of the original Gulf-style architecture, but standing on the waterfront, they are living on borrowed time.

Morning here sees scales fly in the fish market when scores of *houris* sell the still-kicking catch from their nets. Towering above is Arabia's last *baghala:* it is easy to imagine Muttrah harbour in the eighteenth century, flapping ensigns from Basra to Zanzibar.

Muttrah has a real old Arabian style *souq*, with hundreds of dark, cubby-hole shops selling everything from silver needles, used for crocheting skull-caps, to the finest hi-fi sets. I particularly remember

'Martini Henry' muskets in the *souq*. تاجر في سوق المطراح .

one store, its doorway stacked with old 'Martini Henry' muskets and dusty coffee pots. The aroma of rich, cardamon-flavoured coffee percolates the entire bazaar. This, and the ripe scent of sticky *halwa.*

Before the Omani *rial* was introduced, money-changers needed skill to calculate local currency which made a child's sum of arithmetic in the Upper Gulf. At one stage, along with Maria Theresa Dollars, the official currency, they dealt in *rupees, annas, naya peis, pounds, dinars, baizas* — even in solid gold tola bars!

I was scarcely able to handle the simple division of rials. Needing some taxi money from Al Falaj one evening, I asked the night clerk to lend me 4,000 rials, about $8,000, saying I would repay it when the banks opened!

Leaving Muttrah on the Ruwi freeway, one passes the old Mission Hospital, inaugurated by Doctor Sharon Thoms for the Dutch Reformed Church in 1909. As a former nurse myself, it is impossible to imagine how Doctor Thoms and his wife worked without electricity or fans, refrigeration, or proper plumbing. Only a doctor dedicated to God could have stood it.

Oman is still one of the most disease-scourged places on earth, with tuberculosis, leprosy and eye complaints rife. Sultan Said's refusal to permit any Western medicine encouraged the practice of tribal 'quacks'. The shock of some of their grotesque 'cures', such as burning the tongue for consumption, if it did not take the wretched person's mind off his malady often ended his misery altogether. As in some remote parts of the Gulf States, cautery is still common treatment for anything from malaria to malignancy, and I saw Bedouin, both in Dubai and Oman, bearing branding scars.

Eye diseases are the worst affliction. In an interior village I visited, 70 per cent of the population was suffering trachoma and trichiasis, when the lid turns inwards and the lashes ulcerate the cornea.

In 1970, Oman had twelve hospital beds. Today it has over 1,200 with advanced plastic and micro-surgery performed in the Al Nahdha Hospital in Ruwi. Free national health is available to everyone and the strain on the budget is evident when one considers that virtually every member of the estimated 1,500,000 population has something wrong with him. The facilities and staff are overburdened, with the usual reliance on expatriate help.

Under Sultan Said, thousands of Omanis left the country to educate their children abroad. Today, under Sultan Qaboos, the children are running happily to school. On 30 July 1970, in his speech of accession, the young Sultan addressed an illiterate people. One month later, he had established a Ministry of Education in a capital which had only two primary schools.

The fundamental aim is to provide free education for everyone, a programme which has had to be implemented at great speed with little staff and equipment. Requests for schools continue to pour in from remote villages where classes are held under trees and in tents, until the government can provide buildings.

Koranic schools have been encouraged to widen their curriculum and there has been a spectacular increase in pupil enrolment. By 1976, 207 new schools were constructed. A World Bank loan has financed technical and teacher-training colleges and there is discussion about the establishment of an agriculture faculty in Oman, as part of the planned Gulf University.

The impact of oil wealth has seen tremendous progress made in the field of telecommunications. In 1969, there were only 350 telephone lines, today there are 16,000. Oman's 1,000-mile-long coastline, rugged interior and scattered population presented special problems, the solution being found in coaxial cable and micro-wave links. In 1975, the earth station came on beam, Oman's biggest leap of all.

Before 1970 there were no information services; government decrees were pinned on the gate in Muscat. Within a week of assuming power, Sultan Qaboos had a 1 kw transmitter flown in from Sharjah and began the first-ever public broadcasts. Today there is colour television.

Nizwa, the ancient capital of Oman, is reached in a two-hour drive from Muscat. The trip affords interesting glimpses of life in the interior, as distinct from the coast. On either side of the road, villages are perched in the jagged *jabal* which is hemmed in by date plantations.

Date production is still Oman's biggest crop, followed by lucerne, onions, limes, wheat, tobacco, bananas, mangoes and coconuts. Near Nizwa is the government date-processing factory which has a capacity of four tons an hour.

Oman has always been associated with dates, Omanis call them the 'bread of the land' and some tribes refer to themselves as *ahl an-nakhl*, 'the people of the palm'. Every palm is registered and at one time, and possibly still, they were used as dowry. About a dozen varieties of first-class dates are produced.

Nizwa is dominated by a huge circular seventeenth-century tower, and from the parapet one looks down on the maze of roofs of the *souq*, with Ibri's bazaar, the biggest and busiest in the interior. However, having heard so much about Nizwa, I found it disappointing. Apart from silversmiths, its *souq* seemed filled with nothing but butchers, the cold whack of their meat-choppers echoing in the gloomy alleys. Nizwa is a place of sounds, the dull thwop of women pounding sesame seeds inside their houses, buzzing flies and crying children.

Returning to Muscat, we gave a lift to a man who invited us to visit his mud-house in the oasis village of Izki, notable for its very old *al-falaj*.

'Tafaddhal, tafaddhal' (enter), he repeated, ordering his wives to prepare tea and coffee.

The room where we sat was bare save for a vast Victorian stove, and how it got there, or from where it came, is a mystery. We sat drinking on a woven mat, while he waved a palm-frond fan and as we rose to leave, he gave me a bottle of Ribena , saying we would need it for our journey. This is Moslem hospitality. Of all the peoples in Eastern Arabia, I found the Omanis the friendliest and most cultivated. Everyone, from the Ministers to Abdul of Izki, wore an air of quiet dignity.

The main agricultural region of northern Oman is the Batinah Coast, along which one travels to Sohar, north of where it terminates on the eastern corner of the United Arab Emirates. With ample subterranean water, the Batinah is a garden of great potential which, with correct marketing and co-operation from local farmers, could one day supply the needs of the entire Gulf.

The main product is the Muscati lime , whose taste is second to none. Peppers, tomatoes, cabbages, spinach and okra are also grown, while peaches, pomegranates, grapes, apricots, almonds and walnuts flourish in the cooler climate of the plateau – *Jebel Akhdar.*

A current 36,000 hectares of land is under cultivation.

The town of Sib, at the southern end of the Batinah, is where the historic 'Treaty of Sib' was signed, acknowledging the historic and independent way of life of the people of Oman, whilst not granting them independence from Muscat, and prohibiting further assaults on the capital. Dated 25 September 1920 it ended what amounted to civil war.

Sib is still important as the site of Oman's new airport which replaced the old one, in Ruwi, where landing and taking off was reputedly the most hazardous in the world. Twenty-seven miles from Muscat, Sib International Airport has a 10,000 foot runway. It was here that Concorde made its hot-weather test flights.

British Airways fly to Muscat and Gulf Air, which is 25 per cent owned by the Sultanate of Oman, operates to Salalah, capital of Dhofar, the southern province of Oman.

Dhofar

The flight to Salalah takes one over some of the most inhospitable country on earth. More lunar-like than terrestrial, its impossibly rugged ranges flatten out into the barren Wahiba Sands, inhabited by the last true Bedouin in Arabia.

Nearing Salalah, the terrain suddenly changes, as spots of green fleck the *jabal* peaks and surf-lashed beaches fringe a fertile coastal plain. The trip takes only 1½ hours, but it enters another world, for Dhofar is quite different to the rest of Oman.

The 38,000-square-mile province is, with North Yemen, the only region in Arabia to receive regular rain in the tail-end of the Indian monsoon. The 800-foot-high *jabal* behind the coast receives a 30 inch annual rainfall, which gives rise to a temporary vegetation which stretches inland, to end abruptly on the edge of the Empty Quarter, as though snipped off with a pair of secateurs.

Most of Dhofar's estimated population of 150,000 live on the Jurbaib Plain, extending 40 miles north of Salalah. Their activities are fishing and farming, with horticulture catching on, especially copra. The coconuts growing here on tall, slender palms are similar to the Sri Lankan species.

About nine tribes live in the *jabal*. Cattle-breeders, they are known collectively as the *jabali,* speaking a pre-Semitic tongue, inscriptions of which have been found in Himyarite sites east of Salalah, also in both Yemens.

As opposed to the long-headed, hawk-nosed Gulf Arabs, the *jabalis* are quite round-headed, a fact recorded by Ibn Batutta in the fourteenth century. The main tribe is the Qara, who are believed to be descended from Ethiopians, and in whom I noticed remarkable similarities.

One evening two Qara tribesmen sat next to me in Salalah's Bismillah Restaurant. Dark-skinned and handsome, they were bare-chested and wore short black skirts, an end of which was flung across their left shoulder. They came in timidly, like creatures from another planet, and ignoring me, who might well have been a jinn, they laid their flat swords on the table, pulled out chairs and sat wide-eyed in front of the television.

That afternoon I had seen a dozen in the *souq* who, on meeting, had clasped hands and rubbed noses, kissing each other on the cheeks. This sentimental greeting between those wild-haired Qaras is something I will always remember.

The brutal Dhofar *jabal*.

الجبال الـوعرة .

In the first millenium BC, Dhofar's prosperity was entirely due to the unexcelled quality of its frankincense, the precious resin which exudes from the severed bark of the scrabby desert shrub *Boswelia craterii*. The Bait Kathir tribe in the *jabal* owned most of the frankincense trees and usually 'cut' the incense in March, before the humidity of the monsoon.

Milky at first, it hardens into amber 'tears' after exposure. The best is *najdi,* or silver frankincense, obtained from shrubs growing on the desert side of the *jabal*. Although it also grows in the Hadhramaut and Somalia, the finest frankincense comes from Dhofar and all early commerce revolved around its trade.

So far there has been little research into this major economic activity of the ancient world. If oil is the wealth of the present, frankincense was certainly the fortune of the past.

Arabian clay tablets found in Palestine indicate the incense trade with southern Arabia, and the Queen of Sheba's famous journey to Jerusalem in the sixteenth century BC, was possibly to discuss the terms for its distribution – if not for Solomon – whose couch was reputedly perfumed with frankincense.

Herodotus reports that not less than 2½ tons of frankincense was burned each year in the Baal Temple of Babylon. Meetings of the Roman Senate were opened to the burning of frankincense and Pliny reports that Nero burned extravagant amounts at the funeral of his wife, Poppaea.

The major export town was Sumharam, founded by King Iliazz Yalit I, who was known as the 'King of the Frankincense Country.'

Called Moscha by the ancient Greeks, its ruins lie north of the fishing village of Taqah. I was unable to go there as the region had not been cleared of mines one of which killed Andrew Williamson, Oman's first Director of Antiquities, while he was making a journey to research the frankincense trade routes.

Although romantics like to believe in one fabulous overland 'spice route', there evidently existed several arteries with feeder routes. One, via the Hadhramaut, followed the Red Sea coast to Petra, the distribution point for the Mediterranean, and a second, according to Phillips, skirted the Empty Quarter to emerge on the Gulf at Gerra, which is thought to have been adjacent to Dilmun. Phillips made several abortive attempts to find the 'lost city' of Ubar, in the Empty Quarter.

There must have existed a great *caravanserai* somewhere in the desert between the origin and distribution point of frankincense, but as Phillips says, 'a dozen Ubars could well be lost among these high dunes, unknown even to the present-day Bedouin.' His expedition found 'a well-marked highway, centuries-old, made by thousands of camel caravans, leads west...and mysteriously disappears...in the great sands...' Frankincense is no longer a commercial activity, but shrubs flourish around Raykut, west of Salalah.

The Civil War

The story of present-day Dhofar is connected to what was described as the 'secret', or 'forgotten' war which raged throughout the province for ten years until the Sultan declared victory on 11 December 1975.

The harsh regime of Sultan Said was particularly oppressive in Dhofar, where he lived as a virtual recluse, only visiting Muscat once in twelve years! His spies terrorised the Dhofaris and no effort was made to develop its potentially rich agriculture and fishing industries. Fishermen had to pay high taxes for the right to fish and import duties in Dhofar were said to be 300 per cent higher than in the rest of Oman.

When oil was discovered in the Gulf States, thousands of Omanis left, often undertaking the first paid work of their lives. At first many Dhofaris returned to help with the harvest, but their contact with Westernisation in the rich Gulf Emirates sowed the seeds of discontent which led to revolt.

The people had many grievances. The region was backward, and almost forgotten by the world. As late as 1970 there was no hospital, running water or electricity, and the one small school in Salalah had its students personally selected by the Sultan, who had enjoyed an excellent education himself at the College of Princes in Bombay.

Finally, in 1965, the mountain tribes rose in revolt. As not many men were involved, at first the rebellion was not considered serious, but the situation changed when the PDRY (People's Democratic Republic of Yemen) became a Communist state in 1967, with the avowed policy of pushing up through Oman to grab the rich Gulf states.

The PDRY started by taking over the revolution in Dhofar, which was easy, as the Sultan's Armed Forces (SAF) counted less than 300 men. Supplied with Russian money and arms and Chinese advisers, the rebels were quite successful. Many Dhofaris, including women and children, were trained at Hawf, the base south of the border, returning to indoctrinate the others.

When Sultan Qaboos opened his country to civil reform, half the reasons for the uprising were removed, but high in the *jabal* the rebels did not know about the changes, and with the Communists on their heels, they stepped up guerrilla warfare.

Petroleum revenues enabled the young Sultan to expand SAF and pay other countries for their help, notably Jordan, which sent a regiment in 1972, and the United Kingdom. British officers were seconded from UK for two years' service in Dhofar. British pilots were also employed and the Special Air Service (SAS) used to train the *firquat,* or local soldiers, who guard the *jabal* villages.

Contract officers, mainly British, were also recruited. In addition, a British engineering squadron was seconded for civil aid projects immediately new areas were recaptured.

In 1973, Iran sent 1,500 troops with orders to take and keep open the only road between Salalah and Tamarit, or Midway.

In March 1974 a 'Hornbeam Line' of mines and barbed wire was built inland 23 miles from the coast, 33 miles north of the border — an outstanding feat of engineering by British soldiers, working under cover of an Omani-Arab battalion.

The effect of this line was to restrict supplies from reaching the enemy, or *adoo,* in the centre and east of Dhofar. Operations were then accelerated in the *jabal* north and north-east of Salalah, until by May 1975, peaceful conditions had been established throughout the entire area.

Between 1970 and May 1975 about 1,000 tribesmen surrendered. Although no Yemenis were captured, a Dhofari who surrendered when I was in Rakut told me at one time four companies of PDRY regulars were operating inside Dhofar.

In December 1974 the Iranians left the Tamarit Road secure and descended west, to establish another line 68 miles from the border. It is interesting that there is no record of such lines being used, except during the Boer War, but then the Dhofar War was unusual in many respects, since all enemy movement was confined to a very narrow belt in the three-month tree cover following the monsoon.

No major operations were possible during the monsoon, since no aircraft could leave Salalah because of low cloud cover. It was then that the *adoo* moved in supplies by camel convoys, 30-40 animals at a time, slowly plodding their way up narrow passes in the ravines. The biggest weapon a camel could carry was a Russian 122 mm Katushka, and an officer flying with the Sultan of Oman's Air Force (SOAF) told me that they had inevitably bombed many camels.

'It was hard to blast innocent animals,' he said. Five months later he too was dead.

After the May 1975 monsoon, the only *adoo* were west of the 'Damavand Line', so the troops moved west, waiting until the rains ended in October, when, within six weeks, all were driven out. The final village was taken on 1 December 1975, when Dalkut was captured and Brigadier John Akehurst was able to report to the Sultan that Dhofar was secure for civil development.

Especially under a Labour government, British involvement in Oman was always controversial, fanned by the fact few journalists had been there. Together with Swiss broadcaster Madeline Chavallaz, I was the first journalist to visit the war zone after the recapture of Dalkut.

'You cannot say the British won the war when there are only ten British officers in one Omani battalion. It was the Baluch, excellent soldiers who comprise 65 per cent of SAF,' said Lieutenant-Colonel Jonathan Trelawny, Commanding Officer of the Frontier Force. But British casualties of 5 per cent still indicate their proximity to the combat area as this is 2 per cent of the total army strength.

In 1974-5, there were 11 British casualties, three men killed when a SAM 7 missile struck their helicopter, and 25 wounded. Since 1971, the total number of war casualties is put at 200 dead and 600 wounded. Prior to this, accurate figures are not available.

When the Frontier Force took Dalkut, only 27 villagers were there. Most of them were too shy to leave their houses when Madam Chevallaz and I arrived, the first white women they had seen.

A picturesque community of mud and wattle houses, Dalkut lies on a white beach, 30 minutes' flight by helicopter west of Salalah. Its main occupation, sardine-fishing, was interrupted by the war and during the years of *adoo* occupation, nothing was done for its people.

Within 24 hours of the arrival of SAF, food, clothes and paint for the neglected mosque were flown in. A team of exultant men was slapping whitewash on it as we were shown round by the *wali*, or head man, Sheikh Abdullah Mohammed Fatah. A proud-looking man in his early forties, the sheikh had never surrendered, waiting out the war in the *jabal*. He wore a new *dishdasha*, a blue check sportscoat and a flashing silver *khanjar*.

From Dalkut the helicopter lifted us up on to the Darra Ridge which was captured in an exercise code-named 'Operation Halwa'. Here the Iranians were dug in, guarding Dalkut below, and a British engineer was clearing the region of mines.

We did not stay long on the exposed ridge as *adoo* stragglers were still about, especially north at Sarfait and straining my ears, I could hear the occasional sound of mortar-fire pumped over the border.

'They still fire over 100 shells a day, but as it is clear we could go on firing at each other forever, we have stopped and hope they will take the hint,' said Lieutenant-Colonel Trelawny, who saw service in Northern Ireland prior to volunteering to come to Oman. 'Mind

you,' he added, 'in the three years, during which time they have fired more than 120,000 rounds into Dhofar, there have been less than ten fatalities.'

On the eastern side of the ridge, the village of Raykut was also returning to normal. Sardine boats were putting to sea again and its flat-topped houses seemed covered in silver paper with the drying fish.

Because of scorching summer temperatures in the *jabal,* grass survives only 2-4 months after the monsoon, when there is nothing left for the cattle to eat. There exists in Dhofar the unusual practice of feeding them fish fodder in the form of dried sardines which are transported into the mountains on donkeys. Our helicopter carried sacks of fish, and the nauseous smell stayed with me for days.

The area from Raykut, south to the Hadhramaut, is known as 'the coast of a million sharks', and hundreds cruised in the surf as we flew back to Salalah. Once we passed a black slick, like an oil-spill, but it was a shoal of thousands of mackerel, harassed by 80-100 circling sharks.

As I visited Dhofar the week the war ended, few civil aid projects had been started west of Salalah, but in the *jabal* above, schools and clinics had been built and wells drilled, so that life for the Qara and other tribes was also returning to normal. At Hagaif, fifteen miles north, Jordanian engineers and officers of the 20th Field Squadron, a section of the 36th English Regiment from Maidstone, had built a school and sunk a well.

Oman's efforts to win back the loyalty of the rebels by improving social and economic conditions are a lesson to all underdeveloped countries facing the threat of Communism. Having secured Dhofar, the government is endeavouring to bring it up to the same level as the rest of Oman: water-pipes have been laid, a hospital and a new palace for the Sultan built.

There are now fourteen schools in Dhofar, including a boarding school for orphan boys whose fathers were killed in the fighting.

No Dhofari who surrendered — not even 'The Executioner', Said Salim Hof, was ever punished. Former rebels have been elevated to positions of national importance, like the astute young Under-Secretary in the Ministry of Information, Abdul Aziz M. Rowas.

On guard on the Darra Ridge.

جندي عماني في ظفار .

Captured enemy weapons.

مجموعة من الأسلحة أسرت من الثوار .

Education is of vital importance to these Dhofari tribes and the Sultan personally subsidises children 10 rials to attend school. Normally they would be minding cattle in the *jabal*.

Sultan Qaboos told the ecstatic crowd which packed Muscat Stadium for his victory speech: 'Oman is the first Arab country to defeat international Communism on the battlefield. Therefore the Communists will not forget; they will adopt new methods and techniques. Everyone should be on the alert, the soldier on the battlefield, the farmer on his farm, even Ministers in their departments.'

Certainly the Sultan is prepared in the event of renewed aggression. SAF now numbers 13,200 and the navy is 400 strong. Equipment includes patrol boats, armoured cars, scout cars, light artillery pieces — even American TOW anti-aircraft guided weapons, but his biggest investment is in SOAF.

At present this counts 29 Hunter close support aircraft, a squadron of BAC strikemasters, transports and helicopters with a dozen Jaguar low-level strike aircraft, together with 28 Rapier low-level anti-aircraft missile launchers — all requiring British pilots.

Development

As Dhofar is fundamentally a rural region, agricultural projects have priority, with one of the main schemes directed at improving the breeds of mountain cattle.

At Bir Bint Ahmed, good results are being obtained from crossing the hardy, local cows with Friesian bulls, but although the offspring weigh 50 per cent more than local calves at birth, the rate of conception is disappointing. Experiments are now being carried out with Kenyan cattle.

Dhofari cattle stay up in the *jabal,* calving during July and August. So that the people have milk, all bull calves are slaughtered at birth, but the government is trying to discourage the custom by buying the young bulls to fatten until they reach 200 kilos.

On the government farm at Garzaiz, experiments are using Californian Holstein cattle in a project to eventually produce enough pasteurised milk for local consumption.

Dhofar has the richest fisheries potential in Oman, which could be a valuable contribution to its economy and in contrast to the

Officers inspecting an army-built cattle trough near Salalah.

ضباط أنكليز وأردنيين يتفقدون جدول مياه لشرب المواشي . قسم من العمل المدني في ححايف قرب سلالة .

extortion practised by the old Sultan, the government offers a loan-and-grant scheme whereby a fisherman repays only 75 per cent of low-interest loans.

A new port has been built at Raysut, and Arabco Traders of New Zealand has built a 250-ton ice-plant in Salalah and a 3,000-ton cold-store in Muthah.

The problem is that for so long only needing to live off their catch, the men are still only fishing for a basic existence. The influx of Western goods in Salalah will ultimately change their material needs, but, for the moment, fishing remains very much on an individual basis.

Ruled by a strict Sultan, Salalah at one time had all the ingredients of a tale from the 'Arabian Nights', from caravans and frankincense to concubines and slaves. The word 'slave' evokes an emotional reaction and should not been thought of in terms of the wretchedness of life in the West Indies sugar plantations. Most Arabs have no colour prejudice and, however black a slave, they usually treated him as one of the family. A master sometimes raised a slave to a position of great power, treating him as a confidant. Slaves were usually detested by the indigenous population, as they acted in a superior manner and lived in better conditions than they.

If they were mistreated and absconded, however, it was an accepted tradition in the Gulf that they could obtain their freedom by touching the flagpole of the British political agent in Dubai. Today many Gulf state rulers and wealthy merchants employ slaves. They are actually called *slaves,* although 'retainer' is a better description, since to run away from such a good life would be unthinkable. Sheikh Rashid has a dozen or so 'slaves', and is not beyond paying for their university education. The beautifully dressed children riding tricylces up and down the palace hallway in Abu Dhabi were not, as I assumed, the Sheikha's children, but those of her chief 'slave'.

Although Wendell Phillips, who employed slaves on some of his expeditions, says that to be a slave of the Sultan was a great honour, slavery in Oman had more sinister undertones than it did in the Gulf states. Oman was the last place in the world to liberate slaves; Sultan Said reportedly kept several hundred slaves and concubines locked in his palace.

According to Tariq Mohamed Salim Al-Mantehri, Deputy Director of the Southern Area, slaves number 10 per cent of the population. Although slavery officially ended in Oman in 1970, it would not surprise me if many wealthy men of Said's vintage still kept slaves, as opposed to retainers.

Two English electricians I met in the Dhofar Hotel, spoke of seeing 'negro retainers' while they were installing 50 televisions in the new palace. Fifty does seem indulgent of the Sultan, but the proof of his sharing the oil wealth is that they were also being installed in the retainers' quarters.

Salalah's £21 million radio and television station began transmissions on National Day 1975. Prior to the assumption of power by Sultan Qaboos, Dhofar had no radio and only one 50-line telephone exchange, exclusively for the palace.

However, if colour television has moved Salalah into the present, its past still exerts an hypnotic influence in the old palace, where the Sultan spent six years of his life, in the crumbling blue and orange shuttered houses and the gorgeously caparisoned women floating in and out of the heavy, carved doors.

In the *souq* too, though flooded with Western merchandise, there remain shops where wizened tailors sew flowing garments, where tribesmen bargain for bullet-studded belts and everywhere the odour of sardines and drying copra.

Oman's rich history and colourful culture will inevitably lure tourists, when the government lets them in. They will climb the forts of Muscat, browse in the Nizwa bazaars and probably make a special trip to Salalah which the brochure will describe as: 'Romantic, alluring Salalah, where the sun sinks in a blazing ball behind the palace of the wicked Sultan Said bin Taimur...'

It happens like this. As in the Gulf States and all underdeveloped countries seeking status. No doubt a Frankincense Hilton will rise by the sea in Raykut...

6 The Vanishing Bedouin

'...to his conservative nature all change is abhorrent and he can never be driven...Home was the tent and any durable structure an abomination...'
('The Bedu' from *Unknown Oman* by Wendell Phillips.)

The Bedouin, who once comprised 40 per cent of the population of the Gulf States and Oman, have already become folk-heroes for the coastal communities, and although the town Kuwaiti or Qatari may curse a careless driver with the cry of. 'a-aaa *badawi!*', coffee gossip regales their desert sagas. For Westerners, too, the Bedouin encapsulate the romance of the desert. St John Philby, Bertram Thomas and Wilfred Thesiger were all great explorers of 'Arabia deserta', but Thesiger's account of his epic trek in *Arabian Sands* remains the classic work.

I have read and re-read *Arabian Sands,* each time more inspired to follow in Thesiger's footsteps, but while women may now climb Everest, no woman has crossed, nor probably ever will, *al Rub 'al-Khali,* for the Empty Quarter is man's last domain.

Living in the desert, the Bedouin evolved a philosophy suited to their social and economic means of survival, since the life soon separated the strong from the weak and the desert never tolerated fools. The qualities most suited to survival were bravery, determination, self-reliance, honour, vigilance and resourcefulness.

As a race, the Bedouin are outstanding individualists, but alone in the desert an individual stood no chance; thus the infrastructure of desert life was moulded to a tribal society. The tribe was an extended family stemming from a common ancestor, its sheikh, meaning 'old man' in Arabic, chosen by the council.

The sheikh's main tasks were to arbitrate within the tribe, not by dictatorial means, but by his wisdom and personal qualities and to lead it in war. The prestige and strength of a tribe depended on the strength of character of its sheikh.

Although the nature of nomadic life precluded the acquisition of superflous possessions, the sheikh had to be in a better position than the others in order to assume the responsibility of offering traditional hospitality to travellers; if he was unable to entertain a visitor well, word would soon pass round and his reputation would be ruined.

Cherishing freedom above comforts, the Bedouin never owned more than mobility allowed. The same is true today for the few families still clinging to a nomadic life in Qatar, the UAE and Oman: a goatskin water bucket for the family's needs, a bag for making buttermilk, its tripod, the loom, a camel litter, child's cradle, mattress, rugs, coffee-pot and glasses, plates, the tent and latterly, a large transistor radio.

Tents and Cars

The tent was suited to the environment. Quick to erect and dismantle, usually the woman's chore, it was divided into two sections by a curtain, on one side the woman's domain for cooking and sleeping, on the other room for eating and entertaining by the men. The good side of the curtain was invariably turned towards the men.

The tent was never more than what could be supported on three

Bedouin encampment in Qatar.   مخيم للبدو في قطر.

poles, so a man's wealth was not judged by the size of his tents and by the numbers of his herds of sheep, goats and camels. The Bedouin lived off their camels which provided food, clothing and requirements for the tent.

While other Arabs generally consider the Bedouin to be rather godless, it would be inconceivable for them to doubt his existence, since to them God is everywhere, an almost animistic conviction which gave them the courage to endure.

Today they follow Islam; most observe Ramadan and pray regularly, and it is a misunderstanding of their way of life for townspeople to claim their prayers are unacceptable since they don't perform the correct ablutions, according to the Koran. In the desert where men can die for a drop of water, the Bedouin cleanse themselves with sand.

And in the desert, where life consisted of moving from one oasis to the next, the Bedouin were driven in upon their own creative spirit. Poetry and story-telling played an important role in their lives. Thesiger says they loved to talk and that even after the most exhausting day's travel, there was never any peace around the evening campfire, as the same stories were told over and over again.

Music played a lesser role in Bedouin society than among the sedentary coastal peoples. But at festivals and poetry recitals, there was some musical accompaniment, the most usual instrument being the one-stringed violin, or *rababa*, small hand-drums, oryx horn flutes and tambourines. Certainly the music of Qatar is rhythmic, often sweet, stirring a certain fire in one's feet.

Their austere lives afforded little chance for leisure and in consequence the Bedouin developed no Western art forms, although their possessions reveal a geometric influence seen in all Islamic countries, evident in the shape of a buttermilk bag, or the angle of a tent.

Weaving was an art form which evolved of necessity in the cold desert nights, but the flamboyant colour patterns of the woollen rugs made by the women are conscious designs. The kaleidoscopic colours used are strange. How does the neutral-toned desert, inspire the vivid purples, emerald greens and fuschia pinks?

In former times, the various tribes were always fighting with each other. Shortage of food and water led to intense competition for what was available. The constant feuding made every tribesman a warrior and tribal loyalty surmounted all personal feelings. Their indifference to death is now remarkably illustrated on construction sites and in the manner in which they drive motor cars.

In the bare sands, the success of a raid depended on surprise. Raids were planned for months: 'Deny me the right to raid and you deny me the right to breathe' is an old Bedouin saying, but again, there existed a strict code surrounding wars – no enemy could be slain in his sleep and if there was a feud, formal word of warning had to be sent in advance. Relations between the tribes were regulated by conventions based on honour, for which a mean would fight to the death, with alliances, or *ahlafs,* formed, agreeing to fight, or not to fight.

A set of rules also surrounded travellers. Someone who wished to pass through hostile territory would request the goodwill of its sheikh who could not refuse, since this would be shameful. Granted protection, he could safely pass, as Thesiger did, in company of a guard, or *rafiq*. All members of the enemy tribe had to swear to this temporary truce.

Change for the Bedouin began moving across the Gulf as soon as oil wealth brought cars and planes, giving the governments greater mobility than the nomads who had always sought refuge in the sands, confident that no one could follow them. Another blow at their freedom of spirit occurred when definite political boundaries were laid across their traditional migratory paths and central authorities, enforced the peace.

Thesiger writes: 'It is strange that tribal law can only work in conditions of anarchy and breaks down as peace is imposed...since under peaceful conditions, a man who resents judgement can leave the tribe and live by himself.'

Along the Gulf Coast, where tribal structure was changing as a result of Western influence, the economy of Bedouin life was also altered by the imposition of peace. No longer could they pillage caravans to buy the few necessities required from coastal towns, and as foreign trade increased in centres such as Kuwait and Dubai, the Bedouin lost their markets for the simple things they used to sell, like hides and ghee. The car also meant an end to the centuries-old livelihood of breeding camels and the final blow was the discovery of oil.

In the desert, they had led an almost totally self-sufficient existence, particularly the tribes in southern Oman who traded by barter, but even so, they still needed commodities like sugar, coffee and ammunition, whose cost suddenly rose out of all proportion as oil wealth inflated local prices.

The discovery of oil in the Gulf has fulfilled their dreams, and although some Westerners believe that only the ruling class is rich, in the Gulf States money is slowly filtering through to the Bedouin. Money to send their children to school; to build hospitals so they no longer suffer at the hands of 'quacks', and houses with electricity

New housing for the Bedouin.   بيوت جديدة للبدو

and running water. After the terrible desert existence, where life was directed at survival, it is not surprising they are moving into the new towns, like Abu Samrah, in Abu Dhabi, whose social welfare programmes aimed at resettling the nomads are most advanced.

Abu Samrah, one of several new villages along the Abu Dhabi-Al Ain freeway is typical of satellite settlements being built by Sheikh Zayed. It has a mosque, shop, clinic and school surrounded by white and blue cement homes of two bedrooms, a lounge, kitchen, bathroom, laundry, courtyard and garden enclosed by high walls.

Each house is identical. There is a coffee percolator and cups scattered about the kitchen; a double bed plus three or four packed suitcases spilling robes on the floor; a carpet and cushions surrounding a huge television set.

Outside one house when I visited the village, a bearded patriach was watering camels, filling a bucket with a hose. Seventy years old, Mayouf Salim was married to a young, veiled girl who had borne him three children; two of his previous wives had died and he had divorced the other. Raised near Al-Ain, he has lived a nomadic existence until moving into this free government house in Abu Samrah.

Through my driver, I asked if he missed the old desert life? He took a long time to reply, then he answered that his tent had been very old and now he was able to earn some money looking after the village water-pumps. He kept five camels for milk but no, he did not ride them any more as his neighbour had a Land Rover. Himself? He couldn't drive.

'What do you think of the changes in Abu Dhabi and Al Ain, under Sheikh Zayed?' I asked.

'Before, everything was desert,' he said, 'now it's wonderful.'

'What do you like the best? Your house, the water, or the electricity?'

'The television', he quickly replied, 'because every night I can see our ruler, Zayed.'

Salim then asked if we would like to see a Bedouin wedding. Two miles off the freeway, as the car began to labour in the sand, we arrived at a makeshift camp, another clash of West and East, for modern tents were tied to primitive palm *barastis*.

Men sitting in the tent got up and came to greet me, but the women were evidently hidden inside the *barasti*. After shaking some thirty or so hands, I sought to enter the *barasti*, where heaped plates of apples, oranges and dates were spread about, but the heavily veiled women waved me out, which was unusual behaviour from Gulf Arab women, for until now, even the shyest Bedouin had always been friendly. Deciding it might be my cameras. I left them at the door and entered again, hand outstretched and smiling a big 'asalam aleykum'. They stared icily at me through their *burqas*, but I kept my hand out, knowing they could not refuse to take it and finally one did, then the others, half-rising and returning salaams.

It was sad we could not converse, I from the West and these women of the East, for we had so much to talk about. Fruit was offered and a young woman took a large knife and peeled me an apple, handing me the quarters; a servant then arrived with a dish of quivering, orange *halwa*, into which I plunged my hand.

The bride was not present, so I assumed she must be hidden in a small blue tent which was tied to a Range Rover. It was a traditional Bedouin wedding, seven nights of eating and dancing. Nearby, under a twisted thorn tree, a mountainous Sudanese cook stirred huge black pots over smouldering fires.

'Goat?' I asked.

'Camel', he said, and peering over the rim, I saw what seemed to be half a dozen eyes, bubbling in the froth.

Since few Bedouin still live in *barastis,* these people must have come from one of the resettlement towns, like Abu Samrah. The biggest is Medinat Zayed, a hundred miles south of Abu Dhabi and north of the Liwa Oasis.

Until the Bani Yas moved to Abu Dhabi, Liwa was a base between their pearl-diving and date-growing peregrinations — winter in the desert and summer on the coast.

Today, date-growing is still of some importance in Liwa, but many Bedouin have moved out to new homes in Medinat Zayed, taking up irregular work as taxi-drivers, but leaving one family member to keep an eye on the camels and dates — a superficial transition, half-in and half-out of the desert.

Still others have quit the remote, dune-fringed oasis for a permanent life in Abu Dhabi, one of whom is the Moosa family, who told me their thoughts on how the sudden changes brought about by the discovery of oil have affected the people.

The father is 65-year-old Mohomed Moosa, who was born in Liwa, where he cultivated date-palms and kept twenty camels for milk and meat. Like the majority of Liwa's estimated population then of 2,000, he spent the winter there, cleaning and cutting the palms and moving the camels to new pastures. His father was blind and to support his mother and five sisters, he began this work at the age of ten.

After the winter he used to make a camel trek to Tarif to purchase rations for his family during the summer months when he left to work as a pearl-diver; in those days, the journey from Liwa, through the towering, 600-foot-high dunes, used to take him ten days. Working as a diver, he got a quarter-share of the profits, eventually saving enough to buy his own boat.

'Before man forces you to work, you never really know how to look after yourself,' he told me, 'so once I had enough money, I became a *nakhuda.*'

In 1951, when the Saudis invaded Buraimi, Moosa moved his family from Liwa, which is only 50 miles north of the Saudi Arabian border, and joined the defence force, organised by Sheikh Shakhbut, which was stationed at Markhiah. He was elevated to the Emir there

Saayah bin Moosa, Under Secretary for Electricity and Water.

ساېح بن موسى مسؤول في وزارة الماء والكهرباء .

serving five years. In the early sixties, Mohomed moved again, to Abu Dhabi, where his son Saayah began work as an apprentice at the BP training centre, under Michael Daly.

At the time Saayah knew only the Koran, but under Daly's auspices he learned workshop practice and English and his potential was good enough for BP to select him for higher education in the UK.

After graduating from Swansea University with a degree in mechanical engineering, Saayah returned to Abu Dhabi in 1974, obtaining a position with Sheikh Suroor, Minister for Electricity and Water. In one year he was promoted to Under-Secretary, also becoming Daly's partner in a construction business; today the entire Moosa family lives in a middle-class villa in central Abu Dhabi: Mohomed, the father, Hemama his wife, 19-year-old Moza, Saayah's wife and Latifa, their baby.

Seated cross-legged on the gold carpet in their lounge, and with Saayah acting as my interpreter, I asked them about the transition from a desert life.

'Mother says that Abu Dhabi was happier before,' Saayah translated. 'In the old days, she used to cook and visit people but now everyone stays at home, we have lost the old custom of hospitality.'

Wearing full *purdah*, Mrs Moosa waved brown, henna-stained hands as she spoke, her voice rising higher and higher with excitement.

'Will she always wear the *burqa?*' I asked.

'Until she dies,' interpreted Saayah, 'but she doesn't mind if young girls don't wear it.'

'What does she feel most deeply about living here, in comparison to Liwa?'

'It's not for our wealth, that she prefers Abu Dhabi,' he said, 'here she is much more comfortable, but she says she is content because her whole family is around her.'

'Any regrets about the old desert life?'

'Now, when she turns on a tap,' said Saayah, translating exactly what she had said, 'she regrets the years she had to draw water from the well, to fetch the wood for the fire and having to stick her boob in my bloody mouth, when she could have used a bottle!'

While Mrs Moosa paused for breath, Mohomed added his thoughts about the impact of oil on Abu Dhabi.

'If the young people become unstable through drink, not heeding the advice of their parents and wasting the family's money, then the change is not a good thing,' he said.

'I spent ten years in England,' Saayah interjected. 'Sometimes driving my Range Rover through the desert, I feel I would like to return, but then I realise I don't really miss anything about either life. I don't really even like to leave Abu Dhabi,' he said, tugging his bushy, black beard. 'I took Moza to Europe, we stayed at all the grand hotels and went to the best restaurants, but she hated everything.'

Moza, who did not wear the *burqa*, but who kept a black tuille *abaya* pulled over her face, nodded in agreement.

'She had never left Abu Dhabi,' said Saayah. 'She couldn't eat the food and was utterly lost, so when I got a card from my father saying the boat was ready for fishing, I said, "Pack, Moza — we are going home."

'My education overseas did me good. At one time, because of a European girl there, I felt torn between two societies, but I realised I was probably conditioned by the new social environment, so I left her.'

Mohomed, the old date-farmer and diver, now leads a quiet life with Mrs Moosa in Saayah's house, which has a big garden, but no plants.

'We were thinking of cultivating grass and flowers, but father likes to feel the sand between his toes,' smiled Saayah. 'I am well off. Besides my government job, I own a stationery shop, a fishing trawler, a small engineering business and my side of Bin Moosa and Daly enterprises. I have three cars — a Pontiac, a Mercedes and the Range Rover, but yes, there remains something in my heart for the desert. The old life there chasing hares and climbing palms, but I haven't been to Liwa in ten years.'

He looked up from the carpet to the empty light socket on the ceiling.

'I must buy a chandelier,' he remarked abstractedly.

'Why not an ordinary lamp, Saayah' I asked.

'Doesn't everyone have chandeliers?' he said.

It is knowing the desert which draws this generation back, but the more they taste the easier side of sedentary western living, the more difficult their old existence will become for them, and for their children, educated in the free government schools, it will be unacceptable.

So what will happen to the Bedouin as a race? The new generation will be rapidly absorbed into the Gulf's expanding towns and nothing can prevent Westernisation. All the Gulf States are building low-cost housing for the Bedouin and certainly some in Abu Dhabi are as smart as anything on the *Costa del Sol,* and reafforestation schemes are turning the desert green.

Thesiger sees it differently:

...all that is best in the Arab has come to them through the desert — their deep religious instinct...their pride of race...their generosity...their dignity...some people claim they will be better off when they have exchanged the hardship and poverty of the desert for the security of a materialistic world. This I do not believe.

If one classifies the Bedouin as nomads, then as a race they are doomed, and while I believe it is every man's right to education, which is the foundation of civilisation, the tragedy is that the choice is not theirs.

The problems of the Western economies and the high prices of oil produced in their own countries has caused fierce inflation in the Gulf States and it is this economic force, beyond their comprehension, which has driven them out of the sands into the fringe Westernisation of coastal towns.

THE CAMEL

To most Westerners, the Arab without a camel is akin to a cowboy without his horse, but as the Bedouin move into houses and buy cars, and planes land at remote desert airstrips, the camel as a means of transport is finished.

Just as one is unlikely to see a kangaroo in the coastal region of Australia today, so few visitors will come across a camel in the Gulf. Small camel markets exist in Doha and Dubai, and in interior Abu Dhabi they are kept for milking, hobbled beside garages housing limousines; only in southern Oman do camels retain their former status as 'ships of the desert', owned by nomads in the Wahiba Sands area and on the edge of the Empty Quarter, where the twentieth century has not yet made a mark.

Oil wealth and the internal combustion engine have given the camel the same fate as the horse. I went out with a boy in Dubai who drove a Maserati, but his father used to ride a camel in to trade. In fact the original hobbling place in Deira remains and one hears expatriates arranging to meet on the 'sand patch', without realising its significance. From being man's best friend in the desert, the camel has sunk to no more than its market value for hide and meat, which was an inflated $300 for mangy beasts I saw in Doha.

The earliest pictures of camels are seen on Egyptian pottery dating from 3500 BC and bas-reliefs in Persepolis, on the Persian side of the

The camel gives way to the car.   الـدبارة أخذت محل الجمل في الخليج .

Gulf, depict people leading camels to present to the Emperor.

In former times, and still today amongst the Wahiba nomads, the camel was used as a dowry and a man's wealth was estimated by his herd; legend tells of the Arabian potentate Antar Ibn Shaddad, from whom a thousand white camels were asked as a bridal price.

A camel in good condition is a splendid-looking animal, whose points are as much admired by the Arabs as those of a thoroughbred horse by an Englishman. The Austrian scholar von Hammer Pungstall claims to have discovered 5,744 different names and epithets for describing the camel in Arabic.

Ideally equipped for the desert environment, the camel has thickly fringed eyelids which act as a shield against the sand, with a third, transparent lid which is dropped like a blind during sandstorms, and muscular nostrils which can be partially closed for the same reason. Wendell Phillips records the Bedouin story that when the first lonely camel learned that Allah was to create for him a spouse, he smiled so broadly that his nose split up the middle and it has remained so ever since.

Then there are its broad, flat feet which spread out on the sand as it walks, and its hump. The most common myth about this is that it is used for storing water, but it actually is a lump of fat which acts as a useful energy store on long treks. The 45-kilo hump is an indication of a camel's condition, and those of dying beasts I saw in Ethiopia had shrunk to little more than flaps of skin.

A camel can lose up to 25 per cent of its body weight without outward sign of distress, yet in thirty minutes an impoverished beast can swell back to its normal size. It can drink 114 litres in one burst, the water quickly entering the tissues. The stomach is a mass of fleshy pockets filled with a foul-smelling fluid on which it is possible, as has been reported, that a thirst-crazed man could sustain himself for a time.

And while some think of camels as being merely a means of transport and milk, the Bedouin had a myriad uses for them, so much so that they have, with justification, been described as parasites on their camels.

Of prime importance is the rich, salty milk which also makes excellent cheese. The tastiest cheese I have ever eaten was smoked camel milk cheese in Djibouti, but although I enquired everywhere for it in the Gulf area, it seems the Bedouin do not make it there.

Most camels in southern Arabia are she-camels kept for their milk. The bulls are killed as calves. Some English friends in Ras al-Khaimah told me of a Bedouin family who rented a cottage next to theirs in Abu Dhabi and who arrived with a she-camel and calf. To ensure milk for the family, the husband fitted the camel with a type of brassiere, to the chagrin of the calf, and indeed the English people, who were kept awake all night by its cries.

Many superstitions surround the milk, such as if an animal is milked with dirty hands, or into a bowl soiled with food scraps, that her supply will run dry. Mixed with honey and taken for several months, the milk is believed to increase virility and the custom of

Mud houses with television, Buraimi Oasis.

Crumbling tower in Ras al-Khaimah. The Gulf Arabs have not yet thought to preserve their heritage.

Flared gas at Dukhan, western Qatar, will be harnessed in a new government gas scheme.

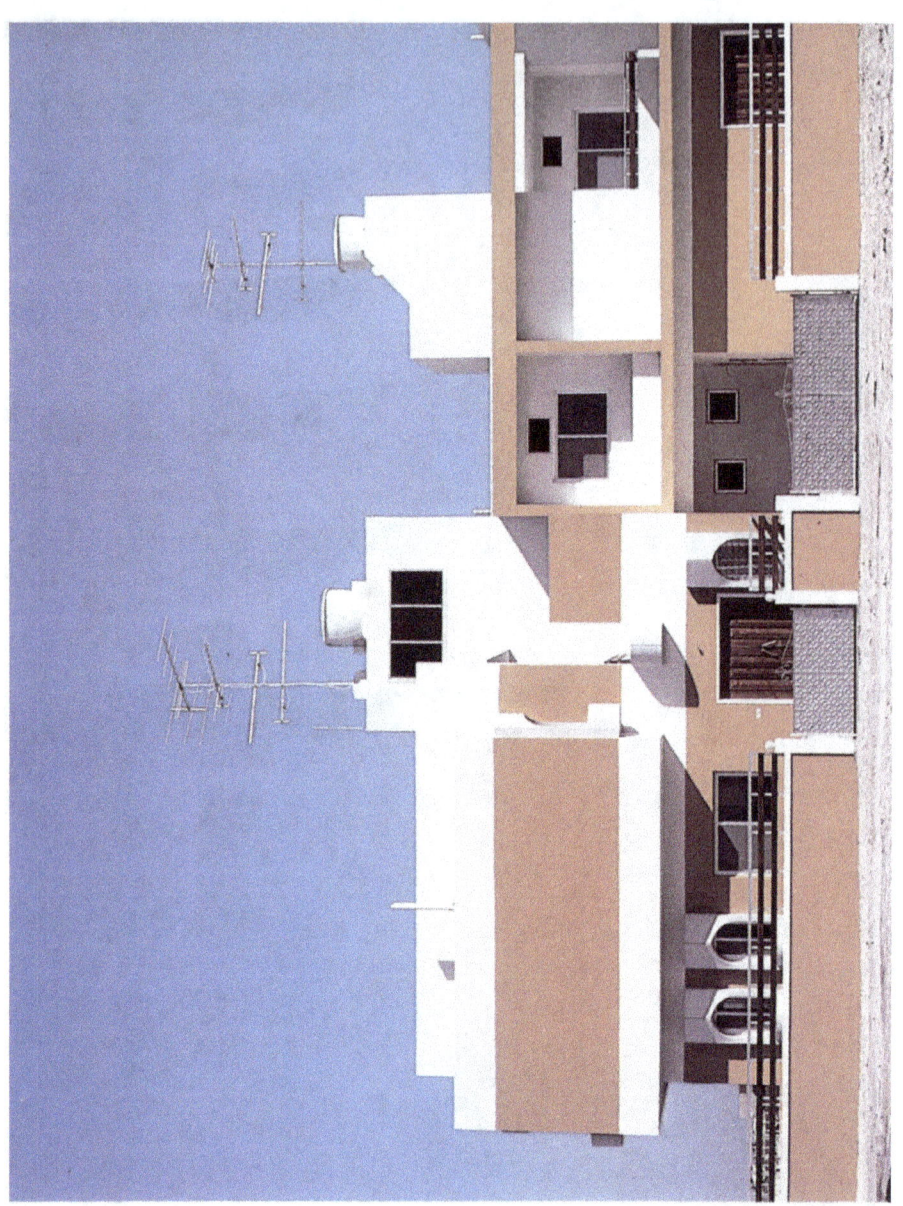

Oil tycoon's house in Abu Dhabi.

Barasti ghetto for Bangladeshis in Dubai.

This scene in Nizwa, interior Oman, illustrates the transition in transport.

The *Masjid Khisru* seen under the full moon in Abu Dhabi.

Date merchants discuss prices in the Nizwa *souq*.

'blowing' a camel's vagina to make her drop milk is still practised by the Qara tribe in Dhofar, who also believe it is taboo for a woman to milk.

She-camel urine is used as a purgative, an antiseptic and, mixed with milk, as a tonic. New-born infants are dipped in it and dusted with the powdered dung which is used for fires and mixed with wattle for building houses. Writer and explorer C. A. Powell reports seeing two Bedouin wash their braids in camel urine whipped up with rotten eggs – surely the ultimate shampoo.

Slaughtered, the camel provides much meat and fat which the Bedouin love. Its hide is woven into belts and scabbards and fashioned into water and buttermilk bags. In parts of Iran and Iraq where the Bedouin still migrate, its skin is used to make their distinctive black tents; but in the Gulf, where the Bedouin survive, tents are woven of goat's and camel's hair, interspersed with white linen, or cotton strips, which give them a striped, zebra-type appearance; camel hair is also woven into *abayas*.

While camels are normally gregarious, hating to be separated from their fellows, unlike the horse, they never show any affection for their master, although they come in answer to their name. Despite this malevolent nature, usually seen in bulls during the rutting season, the Bedouin are normally kind to them, always considering their well-being first and rarely mistreating them. Thesiger says: 'Often I have watched my companions fondling and kissing them while they murmured endearments,' something they would never do to their wives.

Perhaps as a result of the inhospitable desert, the camel is mean-tempered, and has a will of its own. It is particularly surly when roused early for work and the eerie, hollow groaning of a herd is audible for two miles. During raids, the Bedouin tied their mouths, so as not to alert the enemy of an impending attack.

While it will use its feet to effect, the most common way of showing irritation is for a camel to take a slashing bite at the person annoying it. Its upper and lower jaws contain six ugly yellow incisors which can inflict a mortal wound. In Tunisia, I heard of a camel-driver scalped by his beast, while giving a tourist a ride.

Another tale claims camels hate to copulate in front of human beings. Mating camels retire out of sight in the dunes, and if they are surprised by some unsuspecting soul, the male will chase them away. It is also said that if the person manages to escape the camel may spend years waiting for his revenge.

Whether this is true or not is debatable, for Thesiger recounts a different tale, saying that since there are so few sire camels about,

Camel races on UAE National Day.　　سباق الجمال في مناسبة يوم الإمارات العربية المتحدة.

that when one is heard to be in the vicinity, Bedouin from miles around will bring their she-camels to be served and one can hardly imagine them retreating into the dunes, couple by couple.

The female Omani camel, bred on the Batinah Coast, is considered the best breed in Arabia and on soft sand, can cover up to 15 m.p.h. Lawrence once rode a camel 90 miles in 22 hours and Thesiger 115 miles in 23 hours.

In the remaining regions of interior Abu Dhabi and Oman, where camels are still ridden, the Bedouin choose to walk, rather than trot or gallop, since they are always on the look-out for food.

They mount and ride in a special way, grasping the 'tree' on the front of the saddle, whereon, feeling the man's weight, the camel rises off its hind-legs and with another jerk, regains its feet, as he swings himself up. A camel at full gallop is a marvellous sight, especially if the rider is kneeling in the saddle, resting on the up-turned soles of his feet, in which case he is riding entirely by balance.

I had a good glimpse of galloping camels during camel races held in Abu Dhabi on UAE National Day. In Al-Ain, a few days previously, I had seen them heading for the coast and some forty took part in the desert race-track outside town. Although the first race was interesting enough, it soon became boring, as the track was so long that one had time to eat a three-course lunch between the start and finish.

Still, the crowds perched like crows and cockatoos atop cars and petrol-tankers provided colour, while one awaited the cloud of approaching dust. There was also the odd highlight as when one bolted, sending me diving through the rails from where I'd been photographing, to come up under some gentleman's *dishdasha*.

FALCONRY

Hawking is the other traditional sport of the Gulf Arabs, although today's prices for well-trained birds are soaring as high as the falcons. In the forties, a falcon could be bought for about £8, but inflation has upped this to anything from £1,000 for a good hawk. In Doha, the owner asked £5,000 for a *shahin* I admired in the *souq* and a *hurr,* or saker falcon, was priced at £7,500.

Therefore, whereas falconry was once a recreation enjoyed by even the poorest Bedouin, today it has become the exclusive sport of sheikhs. Sheikh Zayed is probably the keenest falconer in the Gulf, followed by Dr Mana Saeed al-Otaiba, whom I met training falcons on the eve of the OPEC meeting. Sheikh Rashid is also an avid hawker. In the fifties he made a hunting trip to Pakistan, taking with him £30,000 worth of falcons.

In December 1976 Sheikh Zayed and his son Sheikh Sultan organised the International Conference on Falconry and Conservation in Abu Dhabi. A hundred delegates from countries as diverse as Arabia and Canada attended the conference. They ranged from Bedouin drivers to English dukes, who all shared a common bond in falconry.

Falcons perched on their owners' wrists.　　المؤتمر العالمي للمحافظة على الصقور في أبوظبي.

That December, everyone in Abu Dhabi seemed to carry a bird on his wrist and, worried about what to do with them, the Khalidia Palace Hotel elected to put all the falcons together, in one of its £43-a-night rooms. 'We had to move them out again', said housekeeper Mrs Penny, 'they sounded like a flock of muffled peacocks.'

The birds favoured for hunting in the Gulf are the *hurr* and the *shaheen,* but honours go the *shaheen,* whose spectacular long-range vision makes it able to sight prey from great heights. A short-tempered bird, especially when it is old, it takes longer to train than the *hurr,* but it flies faster than all species over short distances and its flight movements are very agile. The female flies more quickly than the male, but is less effective in aerial attacks, which are considered the most thrilling part of the hunt.

The natural prey of the *hurr* is bustard, rabbit and plover. It is a patient hunter with great strength, flying faster over long distances and more capable of making a kill. Less sensitive than the *shaheen*, it responds better to discipline, although it is very aggressive when attacking its prey.

Slightly smaller than the *hurr* is the *wukra al-harrar*, which is very aggressive. It is said the Gulf people can even distinguish the two in flight, by the appearance of the wings which point symmetrically downwards.

Some of the qualities looked for in a good falcon are a wide head, robust thighs, flat feet with heavy talons and broad wingspan with pliable feathers.

The ultimate quarry of a trained falcon is the *hubara,* or Lesser McQueen's Bustard, The bustard inhabits Central Asia, but migrates south through Pakistan and the Gulf to escape the northern winter. The bustard varies in size, but generally it is about as big as a small hen turkey. Despite its weight, it can run quickly and rapidly accelerate in flight. Normally it lives alone, or with a small group which converges as a large flock at breeding time. The male has a pouch in its neck which inflates with air during the mating season. Normally the bustard lives peacefully with other species, but it is a jealous bird and will not hesitate to attack. Lying between its tail-end and stomach is a gland which ejects a sticky, bluish fluid which cakes the feathers of the falcon and can temporarily blind it. Therefore, when it is attacked, it attempts to manoeuvre above its assailant, endeavouring to spray it with this substance, known as *tamal.* Aware of this, the falcon attacks from the flanks.

Capture and Training

Falcons are generally captured in Syria, Iran, Pakistan and occasionally on some of the small islands in the Gulf itself.

When one is noticed in an area, a pit is dug in the ground and covered with palm-fronds to resemble a roof, from which is run a cord attached to a live dove.

Taking a supply of food and water, the man then sits patiently in his hide, waiting for the falcon to sight the dove. When it appears, he encourages the dove to flutter and the falcon drops like a stone from the sky, killing it and tearing the flesh.

As a falcon always feeds up-wind, the man slowly pulls the corpse and falcon closer, finally grabbing it with his hand extended, through a hole in the hide. Handling it gently, he stitches its sensitive eyes, passing the fine threads through both lids over the head. Then he slips on a leather hood, or *burqa* which covers everything except the beak. After several days, the threads are progressively removed and the bird is made familiar to its owner, who gives it a name.

The rules for training a falcon are the same today, as when Shakespeare wrote:

Another way I have to make my haggard
To make her home, and know her keeper's call,
That is, to watch her as we watch those Kites,
That bate, and beat, and will not be obedient.
She ate no meal today, nor shall eat;
Last night she slept not, nor tonight she shall not ...
(The Taming of The Shrew)

A skilful owner can train a falcon from the wild state in 30-40 days. Training is by the subtle imposition of his will over the bird's and the use of force will be resisted for when pushed, the falcon seeks refuge in death. While it is being trained, the falcon never leaves its owner, who eats with it perched on his wrist and sleeps with it sitting on a small, toadstool-like perch beside his bed. It is essential the falcon is never separated from its owner and thus one sees them in unlikely places like supermarkets and on planes. Gulf Air requires that anyone carrying a falcon also buys the seats on either side.

The first lesson is to teach the falcon to sit upright on the thick leather, or carpet amulet, which protects the trainer's wrist from its talons. At the outset, whenever the hood is removed, the trainer lets the falcon see he is carrying a piece of fresh meat, to give it confidence.

The second stage is teaching it to attack the lure, allowing it to fly over a short distance, then ever-increasing distances but prevented from escaping by a string attached to soft leather jesses or leggings.

Finally the trainer and a companion take it into the desert. The trainer swings the lure, usually the wing of a *hubara*, calling the falcon's name. Half a mile away, the other man takes off its hood and it darts towards the owner waving the lure, hitting it in one ferocious swoop. The falcon will worry the lure, attempting to eat it and the trainer then produces morsels of meat from between the feathers, to make it think it has actually made a kill.

Sometimes during a hunt, a falcon will pursue its prey far from the hunter, killing it before the party has a chance to catch up. If this happens, it is natural for the falcon, having killed and fed, to leave its prey and escape. If it hears the man calling its name, or sees him waving the lure, it may fly back because of its attachment for him. However, this is a very loyal bird since only a few falcons ever return.

It can also happen that a falcon may take fright during a hunt, or lose its way back across the desert dunes. In this case the owner will camp out all night, calling its name, waiting for it when hopefully it will have been resting, and will respond to the lure at dawn.

Sheikh Zayed spends several months a year hunting in Pakistan, in Sind, near the Punjab border, where the biggest concentrations of *hubara* are found. His retinue is estimated to kill some 5,000 *hubara* annually. By local law, one can only hunt two days a week, but this the Arabs ignore, even to the extent of hunting inside the national parks. It is a very delicate situation for the Wildlife Management Board of Sind, even a political problem, since Abu Dhabi gives Pakistan an enormous amount in development aid.

'We do not know what to do. The Gulf Arabs are killing 5,000-7,000 *hubara* a year and on the other hand, they are developing our country,' said Dr. M.H. Rizvi of the Wildlife Management Board, who attended the conference in Abu Dhabi.

We met at an afternoon tea party, given for the delegates by Dr Otaiba. His palace *majlis* was lined with superb Shiraz carpets, over which plastic sheeting had been placed as protection from the bird lime.

'The Gulf sheikhs have built themselves superb lodges in Pakistan,' Dr Rizvi continued. 'They lack nothing yet they are building us roads; Zayed has built a women's and children's hospital in Larkana and another in Lahore and Sheikh Rashid has also built a hospital and a school.

'Undeniably falconry is a wonderfully invigorating sport,' he continued. 'Sheikh Zayed joins in everything, cooking and collecting the wood and putting up with the cold and discomforts since he loves the hunt. But then the desert is his natural environment. In this respect, wealth has not changed this generation — but it will the next.'

It was during a visit to Dubai that I was fortunate in being taken to a desert camp where a Bedouin chief was training a young bird.

The Bedouin have known how to domesticate birds since early pre-Islamic times, not simply as a means of food, but also for recreation. It is still the Bedouin who are the best at training falcons and it is they who while wandering with their herds, first notice traces of *hubara* in an area and send a message in to the sheikhs on the coast.

A friend, Dubai merchant Ahmed Baker, called for me at dawn and we drove through the rose-coloured dunes, damp with a heavy

This old Bedouin thought the maskless author was a boy.

هذا البدوي العجوز تصوّر أن المؤلفة صبي .

dew, to where a group of Bedouin welcomed us to their camp-fire. I kicked off my shoes and sat cross-legged on the carpet, drinking hot, frothy camel milk, eating dates, and flat Arabic bread dipped in treacle.

As the men chatted, Ahmed translated that the young female *hurr* had cost £70 and that if she proved to be good, the chief would keep her for several seasons. Alternatively, he would release her in the desert.

One would think that freeing a trained 'killer' would have disastrous effects on the few surviving hares and the even rarer stone curlew, or *karawan*, but strangely enough a freed falcon will only kill to eat, although, oddly, it never breeds.

As the day dawned brighter, Ahmed smiled and told me that in the dimness, the men had thought I was a boy. 'The women also think you are a boy,' Ahmed continued. 'All of them wear the *burqa*.'

I stood up and went over to the *barasti* where they were squatted, baking the bread.

'I've told them you're a girl, now I leave you to the ladies,' called Ahmed after me. As my eyes opened in the dark interior, I saw there were five women sitting around me, all in *purdah*.

'As salaam aleykum, kifhalak?' I said, shaking their hands, to which they gave me the ritual reply of 'il hamdilla bkhair,' meaning 'well, by the grace of Allah.'

Suddenly I started, as someone's hand squeezed my breast, but I realised that the women were still trying to pursuade themselves that the maskless creature was of their own sex! Later, in the sunlight, they giggled at their error, but it had broken the ice and one of them actually posed for a photograph; the only Bedouin woman in the entire Gulf to do so.

Now that it was day, the chief picked up his falcon and removed its leather hood. Blinking, she looked about, then suddenly lunged at a chicken pecking near the carpet, restrained only by the cord on her 'jesses'.

'Attam ya da se!' he exclaimed, stroking her head and crooning to her. 'She learns fast and will make a good hunter,' Ahmed translated.

Sometimes a single bird is offered for sale, but more usually ten, even twenty, are sold, roosting together on their *wakers*.

In Doha's *souq* I came upon about fiteen old Arabs, sitting in the shade with about twenty different types of hawks and falcons. Surrounded by cars and building sites, here was a scene from the 'Old Gulf Coast'. Every so often one of the men would stretch out his arm for a falcon to excrete, out of splashing range of his *dishdasha*.

If starved before a hunt, a good falcon can kill up to nine *hubara* on the wing and four on the ground. When it has grounded a bustard, it strikes at the neck with its talons, repeatedly pecking at its eyes.

When the falcon makes a kill, its owner rewards it with the brains, or perhaps the liver, of the *hubara*. The rest is reserved for cooking, the flesh resembling a cross between a chicken and a duck, but more tender.

Before the flow of oil wealth brought the people Range Rovers, the passage of *hubara* was followed on camels with *saluqis* to flush them from hollows in the dunes. When one is sighted, the cord is slipped off the leg of the chosen falcon and it flies 'off the wrist' in pursuit, soaring higher and higher into the sky as the ungainly *hubara* beats its wings in a frantic effort to escape. A good, brave falcon will strike it in mid-air, like a missile, exploding feathers as the stunned *hubara* plummets earthwards for the *coup de grâce*.

COSTUME AND ACCOUTREMENTS

The traditional dress of the Gulf Arabs is familiar throughout the West, varying little, with the exception of Oman. Now too that so many Arabs travel abroad to conferences and on holidays, they have taken to wearing their local attire because of confidence in numbers.

Male Dress

The *dishdasha* is a long, loose gown, normally of fine cotton, although silk is fashionable among the wealthy class. It covers a man from wrist to neck and flows to ankle length, and is usually worn with brown or white Hong Kong leather sandals which have usurped the old camel-skin thongs.

Most *dishdashas* are white, snow-white in fact, and how they stay so spotless in the dust and heat is a mystery, but I have never seen a man wearing a dirty *dishdasha*. When the climate cools, they may wear beige, black or blue, and in the Upper Gulf, where temperatures drop to 45 degrees, these are usually of a fine, lightweight serge material.

Even more typical of the Western image of the Arab is his headgear. The head-robe is widely known as a *ghutra*, or more specifically a *shemagh*, a word of Turkish origin which has rather strangely been adopted into Gulf Arabic, since it has a rich variety of its own words

A traditional Bedouin folk-dance.

meaning a head-dress.

The *shemagh* is usually made of cotton, although in Kuwait a heavier cloth is seen, often in red, blue, green and black checks, as worn by the former 'Trucial Oman Scouts' and today's UAE Defence Force. Often white *shemaghs* are embroidered with flower-like motifs resembling a baby's christening shawl.

It is worn over a *qahfeeya*, a small, crocheted skull cap, and is kept in place by a black, tasselled cord, the *agul* which evolved from the Bedouin; to hobble a camel, its owner always carried with him a piece of rope and when not required, his head was obviously as a good place as any on which to hang it.

In Oman the men wear a turban or *masar* with the stiff, white skull cap or *dumina* underneath. These are often little works of art with never a duplicated design, although the craft may die as Indians are taking to embroidering them on fancy-stitch sewing machines.

The *masar* is wrapped around the head in a variety of individual ways, most of which look untidy and ready to unwind, however, the cotton is stiff and a well-folded *masar* will keep its shape, even when removed.

The other essential accessory to Omani costume is the decorated *khanjar*, which is worn plunged through a silver belt, and which is the centre-piece, over crossed swords, of the Sultanate's coat of arms. While they are by no means as opulent as the *khanjars*, Bedouin men also wear a small dagger thrust through their leather belts. In Oman, cartridges are often worn over the top and the belt may have a *kohl* case dangling from a silver chain, sometimes a tiny silver ear-pick, plus a small leather purse.

For Omani men, appearance is particularly important, not in a narcissistic sense, but because an air of grave dignity is regarded as essential etiquette. In keeping with this the Sultan, like his father, insists that government employees wear official dress of white *dishdasha* and *mashar*. As in the Gulf States, one can only distinguish rank from the quality of the material and the rich embellishments on the *bishts*, or cloaks, although royalty can never be mistaken as the edges of the *bishts* are always lavishly embroidered in gold, none more so than Sheikh Isa's robes.

Womens' Costume

The traditional costume of Arabian Gulf women remains the black *abaya*, or cloak, which is worn over an embroidered satin shirt of various colours and with baggy satin trousers, fitted at shin level.

Her most famous accessory is the *burqa*, a shiny black, slightly stiffened cotton or silk mask, which covers her face to the hairline, extending over her nose like a sharp beak so that the mouth, too, is not seen. The *burqa* has nothing of the feminine allure of the beautiful blue, black and mauve, lace-edged veils worn below the eyes by Moroccan women; it is hard and cruel-looking and unless it fits quite snugly, her best feature, her beautiful brown eyes, are hidden.

But while the men show no inclination to discard the *dishdasha*, all liberated Gulf women wear superb Western clothes under their *abayas* and many girls in Kuwait and Bahrain have dropped traditional dress altogether.

The dress worn in Oman is quite different, being rich and colourful, in keeping with its cultural roots since located on the trade routes, slaves and merchants have all injected a foreign influence in costume, especially in Dhofar.

Dhofari women wear the most extravagantly coloured and embroidered robes. Their dress is tent-shaped with wide sleeves, a square neckline and a hem which tips higher up in the front than behind, revealing blue, black or red satin embroidered trousers. Over this they fling one, or several, multi-coloured cotton rectangles whose design resembles the *kangas* worn by women on the Kenyan coast, patterned in flowers, or edged in cabbalistic symbols.

The mask, or *shobka*, in Dhofar is drawn right across the face, usually black and gold embroidered net, not quite concealing a white-toothed smile. The children too are dressed in the shiniest, gaudiest of satin brocades fashioned into dresses, jackets and bonnets, edged with gold stitching.

Jewellery

Jewellery is inadequate to describe the finely worked, heavy silver accoutrements worn by Omani women and the Gulf States Bedouin, for many of the pieces have a utilitarian rather than an ornamental use. Silver measuring cups and containers for *kohl*, the eye-liner, and perfumes, occasional talismans like the 'Hand of Fatima' and necklaces, from which are suspended tiny cases containing verses from the Koran.

The most eye-catching jewellery is worn by the Bedouin in Oman, where it is struck by Nizwa silversmiths from melted-down Maria Theresa dollars. Starting with the head, they often wear a delicate silver chain following the central parting in the hair which ends in a silver disc, or crescent, dangling on their forehead. The ears are pierced with large and heavy pendants and occasionally a fine silver chain crosses the forehead and runs under the chin.

A custom which seems to be peculiar to Oman and Dhofar in particular is for the nose to be pierced with a thick gold ring. I saw many women wearing quite large padlocks in their noses, round and square locks, no two alike and occasionally set with what appeared to be jade, but no woman would allow me to photograph her.

Perhaps the most spectacular item of jewellery worn is the *mezzrad*, which consists of a number of silver dollars linked by hollow, ovoid beads, often with a large, intricately designed central

Bedouin girls wearing typical jewellery.

الرقص الشعبي

disc. These necklaces are usually worn by very young girls and are obviously family heirlooms.

In Izki, in interior Oman, I was once startled by a woman who passed me in the *souq* wearing a superb ovoid silver necklace, but what caught my gaze, and sent me racing after her, was a fiery central stone which resembled a giant ruby. When I reached her and said good afternoon, how was her health and her husband's health and her children's health and that 'inshallah', my own was still remarkably good, I pointed to the necklace, which she slipped off and I saw my 'ruby' was an antique motor-car reflector, backed with solid silver!

Silver bracelets are usually worn in equal numbers on each arm and are of two distinct types: a flat bangle with raised spikes and a larger doughnut-shaped *zunud,* always hollow and often filled with pebbles, so it rattles. Similar *nattlers,* or anklets, are also worn by young girls in Oman, up to the age of ten or twelve when they marry; Dhofari women often wear them hung with little bells and in a sandy street, where steps make no sound, one can hear someone approaching by this magic jingling.

The silver rings are especially interesting, each with a special name and worn on a particular finger. The *haiza,* a tiny ring with a cluster of small bearings, is worn on the little finger, the ring for the wedding finger is round, containing a coloured stone, usually of no value, but sometimes turquoise or coral, the *khatum abu fuss* is a flat ring, patterned in noughts and crosses design, which is worn on the middle finger, a sharp inverted triangle ring is for the first finger and the *buthan* is worn on the thumb, a thick, broad ring, similar to those for the toes. Whoever wrote 'rings on her fingers and bells on her toes' must have modelled it on the women of Oman and the Arabian Gulf.

Antiques

It is this silverware and jewellery which is most sought after by visitors and local expatriates, though even in the smallest, dustiest, most off-the-beaten-track shop, the owner will know today's exchange rate on the world silver market.

There is only one place I know where one can buy silver without its being weighed by a cross-legged and frequently cross-eyed little merchant, hunched over a pair of scales; in al-Ain, an old Omani hangs about the museum with a sack of silverware over his shoulder, like Father Christmas,

Oman, from where he buys it, is the most expensive place for silver crafts; a *khanjar* costing £60 today, even a new one. The silver-embossed 'Martini Henry muskets' which tempt most men should be viewed with caution. Most are still in working order and as such are regarded as firearms. The only way to get them through airport security is to bore a hole in the beautiful barrel; a good rifle costs upwards of £120.

For old jewellery and other desert bric-à-brac, there are many shops in Muttrah *souq*. There are several antique shops on the perimeter of Dubai's gold market. The best is painted blue and is owned by an old, hookah-puffing Arab whose father was a slave in Persia. Sharjah has little to offer in the way of antiques, since most were bought by the departing British.

When I first went to the Gulf, one could buy old coffee-pots and copper bowls at absurdly low prices since the shopkeepers, avaricious for the flood of Western goods, did not comprehend their value to a European. Even recently, a driver helping me sift through the rubble in a Sharjah shop kept asking why should I buy such a dirty, dented old coffee-pot when even he had an electric percolator. But in that twelve months, the shopkeeper had woken up and I now paid DH40 against DH15.

Apart from old jewellery, the best buy in the Gulf states is a coffee-pot, if any are to be found; again Muttrah *souq* is suggested and the small market adjacent to Buraimi.

There are many different types of coffee-pots, and the oldest are usually copper-banded in tinned silver with a peaked lid and spout, filigree work and hooks dangling off the upper lid. Plain brass coffee-pots are also sought after, their origin identified by the small trade mark of the maker.

A final, cumbersome souvenir is the brass-plated and studded chest, loosely called a 'Kuwaiti chest', possibly because hitting the oil jackpot first, the Kuwaitis were the first to throw them out. Before oil wealth bought them furniture, the Gulf Arabs furnished their homes with carpets and cushions, except for clothing and other possessions which were stowed in a chest, a present from the husband to his bride for her trousseau.

The most common variety of chest is covered with solid, brass-patterned sheeting, its lid fitted with a large, ornamental brass hasp and staple, to which a padlock was attached.

An interesting feature on some of these chests was a primitive type of burglar alarm device, where it was impossible to turn the key without activating a small, sprung hammer which struck a bell and presumably woke the household. Many chests had several concealed compartments and drawers.

There are four places where one can see such chests today, in the homes of old Gulf coast personalities such as Dame Violet Dickson, in the Dubai Museum, rotting in the streets of Muttrah *souq* and in Mombasa — most of Kuwait and Oman's most beautiful chests were traded for slaves, in East Africa.

7 The Emerging Women of the Gulf

Enjoin believing women to draw their veils over their bosoms and not reveal their finery except to their husbands...fathers... husband's fathers...sons...step-sons...brothers...their women servants..., and their slave girls; male attendants lacking in natural vigour...And let them not stamp their feet in walking so as to reveal their hidden trinkets...(The Koran)

Liberation, in any form, arises from an awareness of social oppression and an understanding of what is wrong, and what is wanted. Ability to bring about the desired changes stems from education, so that where there is a large, illiterate population, the need for change is unlikely to be seen. Education also means the availability of money to build schools, but before oil brought wealth to the Gulf, there were few public facilities of any kind, not only because the people were too poor, but also because there were few permanent settlements.

Not only in the Arab Gulf States, but in many underdeveloped nations, women face enormous hurdles to emancipation and, as in the West, 'women's liberation' movements are catching on.

Most Westerners have no idea how Arabian women suffer, not simply from daily masculine tyranny, but also because of tribal superstitions and beliefs: such is the sad custom of 'salt packing' in the United Arab Emirates, done from a fear of divorce when, after bearing many children, a woman can no longer satisfy her husband. This is the ultimate sublimation of woman to man and in such places, 'love' as it is known in the West is rare, and any affection among the new 'oil generation' is in defiance of the system.

During my journey through the Gulf, I endeavoured to learn the truths behind the mysterious black *burqa*. Other Western women writers have interviewed Egyptian, Lebanese and Palestinian expatriates employed in the Gulf States, but I only spoke to native-born women of whom 90% still do not work. I discovered that gradually the new oil wealth is helping them achieve emancipation.

Progress is necessarily slow because custom and Koranic law have both conditioned women to accept a very restricted life. In many places it is the women themselves who insist on wearing *purdah* out of habit and shyness. However other customs, like arranged marriages, are increasingly being rejected by the younger generation.

Kuwait

Kuwait has a strong women's movement which was represented at the International Women's Conferences in Mexico, Berlin and Brussels. Its most vocal supporter is 40-year-old Fatima Hussain, director of Kuwait's only television programme for women.

'As I love my country, I must have the right to vote. Kuwaiti women will get more life when they can vote; it will take their minds off superficial things such as clothes and interest them in more important issues,' she told me.

A mother with three children, Fatima became Kuwait's first woman journalist in 1960 when there were still no papers and the government did not employ women. In 1962 she pioneered a women's radio programme, switching to television in 1963 and today her show, 'Fatima Hussain with the Family', deals with social and domestic topics. She has also published a book of her grandmother's old Kuwaiti recipes, as she is concerned that with all the foreign influences in Kuwait, pure Kuwaiti cooking may die out.

Over lunch she described how things had changed in recent years. 'You know that I wore *purdah,* until I was 23? We used to leave Kuwait in the *abaya* and take it off on the flight to Cairo, then coming home for holidays, we would put it on again! One day, accustomed to not wearing it for two years in Egypt, I decided to abandon it. Everyone was shocked when I arrived at the airport, but I did not give them a chance to comment. They soon saw I was no different, although one day my mother did say — "If only you wore your dresses just a little longer Fatima — people will not talk".'

After lunch, we drove her daughter Nada to ballet lessons in the basement of Fatima's beauty salon, 'Al Zahra'. 'My friends criticised me for opening it. They maintained I should do something more cultured, but the thing is, I make most of my television contacts here,' she smiled.

'Do you have problems getting the more conservative Kuwaiti women to appear on your show?' I asked.

'Oh yes, I have never been able to interview anyone wearing the *burqa.* They refuse to be photographed. I should tell you I was censored last week for saying that women should be allowed to vote and sit in the National Assembly. I am so proud my country is developing as a democracy, but so sad there are no women to help.'

The next woman I met was 25-year-old Suad Essa Yousef, an artist who held Kuwait's first one-woman exhibition in 1974. 'Our traditions make life difficult for an artist,' she told me. 'I like the spiritual feeling of the desert and I want to spend a month there, thinking and painting, but I am not courageous enough. I don't mind being alone, but people would not understand.'

Suad was educated in India and at art school in London. After studying print-making in Chelsea and teaching art at the teacher's college in Kuwait, she is now sponsored by the Ministry of Information, which provides her studio and an income of KD258 a month.

'I like working here in this cool, old traditional house,' she said, showing me her colourful prints, 'Part of me cannot accept the new Kuwait. There are other problems too — a woman artist cannot have her own studio. If she is single, she must live at home with her family as custom decrees. After spending my formative years abroad, I find this difficult. In Europe you are enveloped in distractions, but in Kuwait, you must always seek them out and for a single woman, social life is always in the company of other women.'

Suad's friend is Fawzia al-Sayegh, the paediatrician at Al Sabah Hospital. As her country's first female doctor, 28-year-old Fawzia is something of a 'golden girl' in Kuwait, and I asked what her mother thought of her?

'She is very proud of me,' Fawzia flashed a smile, 'for a Kuwaiti woman she has a progressive mind, like sending me away to study, when I was only 16.'

After graduating from school in Kuwait, Fawzia studied medicine in Cairo, completing a post-graduate course in England, and writing her thesis on gastro-intestinal problems in Kuwaiti children.

'People imagine that because Kuwait is rich so our children must be fat and well-fed. In fact many kids are dehydrated and malnourished.

'The main cause is poor management by the mothers, some of whom may be only 13 and many of whom have never been outside their tent. Normally Bedouin breast-feed up to the age of two or three years and since boys are more revered in Arabia, they are breast-fed even longer. Therefore, since they are not getting any solids, many suffer *marasmus,* a total diet deficiency seen in 50 per cent of our admissions.

'Many also suffer from dehydration because of the extremely hot climate; gastro-enteritis is another common complaint, not from

flies, but again through maternal mismanagement. Schemes are being implemented to educate the Bedouin women in child-care, but in my opinion, the government is not doing enough.'

Fawzia has seven sisters and brothers, and like Suad, as a single girl, she lives with her family. Her unmarried brother is family head, since her 74-year-old-father lives with his third wife.

'I have only been back in Kuwait four months and it is taking time to adjust to our traditions again,' she continued. 'At a recent party, I was the only Kuwaiti girl who danced and when my mother asked why, I explained it was something natural I had done with my Western friends; she accepted it. I have never worn the *abaya* and I smoke, a lot, as you see!

'At present I am not considering marriage, but I see no problem in combining it with work, but to keep my mother happy, of course I must marry a Kuwaiti. Here we cannot go out socially with men and it's only okay to have a friendly situation with someone, if the family is present. Kuwaiti men travel a lot, but they still mind traditions,' she wrinkled her nose.

'The family unit here is very strong and no matter how happy a single girl is in her career, it is considered shameful for her family if she does not marry.

'These things apart, Kuwaiti girls lead a very easy life and are very spoiled. Most get money from their fathers and we would never consider marrying someone, unless he first built us a house and filled it with furniture and servants.'

'But what happens if she says "no" after all this?' I said, slightly aghast.

'I said "no" myself,' she laughed, 'he has it for the next one.'

Later she showed me around the hospital. Nurses greeted her simply as Fawzia, many complimenting her on a recent television appearance when, in the middle of a conference, she had attacked the government for not providing adequate funds for public health.

Bahrain

Although Bahraini women once endured all the customs prevalent throughout the Arabian Peninsula, today, with Kuwaiti women, they are the most emancipated on the Gulf. One of the main reasons is Bahrain's long association with foreign traders and, being a small island, there was more contact between the coastal and village peoples.

It is therefore a little unfair to compare Bahrain with backward

Fawzia al-Sayegh, Kuwait's first woman doctor.

بنات من البدو .

states like Fujairah, where no oil has been discovered and where education is only starting.

Bahraini women lead other Gulf women in many fields; 1972 statistics showed 718 teachers registered and 55 secretaries. Few young women wear *purdah* and even the Emir's wife, Sheikha Hassa, wears Western dress when she travels abroad.

Sheikha Lulua, the Emir's smartly groomed sister-in-law, is a tireless charity worker for the less fortunate women of Bahrain. An animated lady in her early fifties, she is president of the Children and Mother's Welfare Society, which was founded in 1960 to liberate ladies from a life of absolute domesticity.

A main function of the society is sponsoring poor families and widows. 'In particular widows,' said the sheikha, 'so that they can come to us after a bereavement, knowing someone cares. I am a widow, a grandmother too, since I married at the age of twelve. I don't see myself remarrying. I feel I did my bit for my late husband and family and now I am free to travel and enjoy social work.'

'We have also established two kindergartens, and to mark 1975 Women's Year, we extended our effort at liberating women's minds by starting handicraft courses. We also hosted an American fashion show with profits going towards a school for the handicapped.

'We often travel abroad as a group. Forty of us recently went to Spain, without our husbands. Many people were amazed. "Where are your husbands?" they asked. "We don't need them," we replied. One husband even gave his wife the money, saying, "Here, take it, it's women's year, so go!"'

'Is your society working in any way to liberate the lesser educated women from old traditions, such as *purdah?*'

'You would be surprised how many husbands would be happy to have their wives appear unveiled; it's the women themselves who retain the custom.'

'How do you feel about a girl who chooses a career in lieu of marriage?' I asked.

'Certainly today many Bahraini girls are working in shops and as secretaries, but I personally feel sorry for unmarried women, they have their freedom, but the family unit is important. Still, I feel equally sorry for unmarried men. Who will take care of them when they're old?'

'That's where your society could come in.'

'Ah,' laughed the sheikha, 'we are not at that stage yet!'

Maymooma Bastaki, aged 27, is one of the career women mentioned by Sheikha Lulua. She runs a florist's shop in the Gulf Hotel, given to her by her father. 'Many of my friends are working in shops and as secretaries and nurses,' she said. 'His Highness, Sheikh Isa, ordered 11,000 flowers for his daughter's wedding.' she said of what was obviously a thriving business.

'Bahraini women are not narrow-minded, they are advanced in their thinking, I would say even more than the men and compared to the other Gulf States, we are fifty years ahead in education.'

'Believe me, although strictly speaking there is no longer a dowry, no father would ever hand his daughter over for nothing. Yet although most of our marriages are still arranged, I would claim they are more successful than those in Europe. No Bahraini has more than one wife any more and certainly no mistresses. That's for the West. Ninety-nine per cent of women are faithful too.' She watched a group of air hostesses passing the window.

'But what of the sexual inequality in the Koran, whereby a man can divorce his wife, merely by saying so three times?' I asked.

Maymooma did not reply at first, but fiddled uncomfortably with the yellow ribbon around her hair.

'For a women to get a divorce,' she finally said, 'she must visit the *mullah* and explain why she wants one. He will then give her husband three chances to stop the drinking, beating or whatever it is, and should it continue, then she can divorce him. But no matter what the circumstances are, if she asks for a divorce, he has the right, and usually will, to ask for the dowry back, plus any money he may have given her.'

'However, Bahraini men are basically faithful, very sensitive and affectionate and our way of thinking is live and let do, yet despite this, being a tiny island, people gossip. I would never go out with a man unless I was officially engaged and the idea of a boy ringing you for a date is unheard of.

'Bahraini businesswomen do travel alone, but not even in Sydney would I accept to even have coffee with a man. You never know, a Bahraini might pass and your reputation would be ruined.'

'So, despite the fact you wear Dior clothes, run a business and drive a Mercedes, you are still not totally liberated, because of your customs?'

'No. We are Bahrainis, yet we understand a Western girl's ways because we are liberated in our minds.'

'But haven't you the strength to be utterly sure of yourself, knowing you are not breaching any custom, that you don't care what people say?'

'No. In Bahrain it is live as the others do,' she concluded.

Qatar

As has been noted, Qatar is the most conservative Gulf State, where the majority of women still remain inside their homes.

Now, however, with massive oil wealth and an enlightened ruler, an ambitious education programme is under way, with the number of girls attending school today exceeding 14,000, compared to only 50 twenty years ago.

Into the puritan environment of Qatar in the forties was born Noura Kassem al-Darwish, one of the twenty children of the wealthy al-Darwish family, who amassed a fortune from pearling.

'Step by step is better than jumping. We will have everything in time,' she told me.

Qatar's first women inspector of schools, Noura Kassem, no longer wears the *battoola,* the gold- or silver-bordered black mask worn by most Qatari women, but she still throws an *abaya* over her chic Western clothes.

'Custom decrees I continue to wear it,' she explained, 'as you need a passport to go from country to country, so we need to wear an *abaya,* from house to shop. But you can wear it in a very sexy way,' she added, wrapping it round her 'This is silk, but if I have to pass men in the street, of course I wear a heavy one, so nothing is seen.'

Noura Kassem was the first Qatari girl to complete secondary school, after which she graduated in Arabic literature from Kuwait University. Returning to Qatar in 1974, she was immediately appointed girls' school inspector, since there was no one else. 'At first I worried because I lacked the teaching experience, but then I decided as the only qualified Qatari, that I had to succeed.'

Still single, Noura Kassem has strong views on social life and marriage in her country.

'The thing you must understand is that here in Qatar, old traditions persist and you still cannot meet a man, before you marry him. Slowly, though, there is a growing gap between young people who refuse this and their parents. Happily our parents can no longer force marriage on us, but it is still impossible to know a man, because we are not allowed to meet. I personally will not marry unless I have spoken to the man; otherwise it is love by chance. My dearest wish is to see Qatari girls and boys sitting talking on the same divan.'

'How long do you think this will take?'

'You can't see time in days, or years,' she replied seriously, 'it's a big step, but if you study Qatar's history, you will see we have already done so much, so quickly.'

'The Qatari girl is educated, modern-thinking, and she knows what she did, and what she will do. She understands the customs too; thus it is not wrong that we still cover ourselves,' she indicated a group of heavily veiled women passing her office.

'For this you can be sure that any woman wearing a bikini here is not a Qatari. Neither do we drive. It is not prohibited, like in Saudi Arabia, but it is symbolic of our past. I have a chauffeur, because if I drive, it means I change my whole way of life. But something the government must change is the women who still have 'In Purdah' stamped in their passport, in place of a photograph. Obviously this means anyone can use anybody's documents. No! You can't take any pictures of me,' she said, 'my father would not allow it.'

Noura Kassem lives at home with some of her twenty members of family by her father's first marriage. He has two wives. Life is restricted to family outings and women's gatherings, at home. Never in public.

'If I swim,' she said, 'it is in a private pool. No, I have never swum in the sea, but this is not important.'

I felt especially sorry for Noura Kassem. Part of her is willing to change, but the other part is too conditioned by her surroundings to dare. She is, however, making a stand against the system, and once more girls have the courage 'women's liberation' may even emerge in Qatar, with Noura Kassem al-Darwish its likely leader.

Abu Dhabi

Sixty-five-year-old Sheikh Zayed of Abu Dhabi has had a total of nine wives, but today he lives with only one, his last and favourite wife, 30-year-old Sheikha Fatima.

A former barefoot Bedouin girl, Fatima became queen of his desert sheikhdom at the age of thirteen. Even today, no man except her father, her brothers and her husband, Zayed, has ever seen her face and even in the palace harem the sheikha wears the *burqa*. She has never been shopping, to a restaurant, or a cinema, and although she goes to London in the summer, she never leaves her home in Bolton Gardens, except to catch Sheikh Zayed's private VC10 back to Abu Dhabi.

I visited Sheikha Fatima in her palace, the doorway guarded by a stuffed tiger and a lion, its elegant *majlis* lined with cream and gold chairs and divans, with rich Persian carpets covering the floor. Chandeliers tinkled in a breeze through open windows and at one end of the room, a large colour television screened an American Western.

Servants entered, placing juices and chocolates on marble side-tables, more of the sheikha's friends and relatives arrived, her Egyptian secretary Hyatt and finally Her Highness herself, dressed in a cream satin diamanté robe.

Tall and voluptuous, she extended a hand, its fingers dyed with henna and charged with tiger-stone rings. More tiger-stone bracelets encircled her wrists, together with a ruby-faced, diamond-studded watch, while from her throat dangled a tiny gold Koran. As any Western woman might, she wore denim wedge-heeled sandals, but her face was hidden behind a black silk mask.

Beautiful and alert eyes met mine as she too summed me up. Then they crinkled as she smiled a welcome, motioning me to sit on the couch.

'Ahlan awasalan', she said, as Hyatt began to translate.

This young woman has taken the biggest step by far of any woman in the Gulf, literally out of a tent and into a remarkable palace. Yet despite her overwhelming wealth, the sheikha has not forgotten the women from her humble background and she is known throughout the UAE for her benevolence and enlightened work as President of the Abu Dhabi Women's Association.

The association was formed in 1973 by twelve women who wanted to do something for the development of their country. It now has over 300 members who teach illiterate desert women hygiene and handicrafts. As President, the sheikha attends its meetings, but this is the only occasion she leaves her palace.

'We are publishing a women's magazine,' she spoke in softly flowing Arabic interpreted by Hyatt. 'No, I will not have my picture in it,' said the sheikha, slightly irritated, 'I have never had my photograph taken and I never will. It's the work that matters.'

One of the main tasks of the association is to encourage women to attend classes and where her family or her husband objects to her leaving the house, a member of the ADWA will go and talk the matter over. Interested in the progress being made for Abu Dhabian women, Sheikh Zayed donated a special school for such women and to date, some 50 have reached fourth grade.

'Most women here like to marry, but they are not chasing it,' said the sheikha. 'We have much stronger family ties than the West and I cannot see a UAE girl ever preferring a job to a husband.'

On a previous visit to Dubai, I noticed young girls from the ruling family wearing very *décolletté* dresses, a striking contrast to their mothers, in full *purdah*. I asked Hyatt what Sheikha Fatima thought, perhaps that the new 'oil generation' had gone too far, too suddenly?

'Although the UAE is a nation of seven states, some of them have been longer in touch with the West than others,' she replied.

'Are you blaming the West?'

'No. We are trying to adopt the good habits of the West,' said the sheikha.

'What does Her Highness think of bare-top bathing? She must have heard about it, in a place such as France?'

'It is their custom and their freedom,' Hyatt translated her reply. 'Because Europe is so old and it has been doing the same things for so long, it now seeks something different.'

'Could you ask the Sheikha if she sees the day when perhaps no woman in Abu Dhabi will wear *purdah,* maybe not even herself?' I asked.

'Everything is possible. The *burqa* is not law by the Koran, it was only adopted by women in the tenth century. Who knows? Some of the new generation may well want to wear it,' said Sheikha Fatima philosophically. 'I have worn the mask since I was fourteen and will always do so,' she continued. 'It is traditional and I am proud to keep my country's customs.'

'Most Westerners who visit your country try to observe your customs, but there seems no attempt by the Arabs to adopt Western habits, when they travel abroad. This was evident to many people last summer in London when some Arabs were leaving their hotel rooms in a disgraceful state, even brewing coffee in the streets of Mayfair.'

'I can only say that this depends on an individual's upbringing,' answered the sheikha. 'Even though we employ servants and gardeners, before we leave, I check everything myself as I would be horrified to leave it dirty.'

'Sheikh Zayed is on record as saying that God made two sexes to share everything in life. In my travels, except for restricting customs, I have found the Gulf women to be more broad-minded, even more intelligent, than most men.'

'It is true,' replied the sheikha. 'I have eight children and my girls can go to university, if they wish.'

'If women are to be equal in every way to the men, does Her Highness not think they should be permitted to have four husbands, as the Koran allows a man to have four wives? I cautiously asked.

'If a man divorces his wife, it is her fault, since it is her job to keep him happy,' she said perversely. 'Do you have many divorces in Australia?' She looked me straight in the eye.

'Yes, because of the laxness in Western morals.'

'This is exactly why Arabian women must go forward, but at the same time not throw away all their habits and traditions,' said Sheikha Fatima, rising and shaking my hand.

Oman

'There is no future but marriage for any woman of Oman...Arab women are the downtrodden, mindless slaves of their fathers, brothers and husbands...by 28 the majority are old and worn-out grandmothers sorrowfully facing an early death,' wrote Wendell Phillips in 1966.

The story of 'women's liberation' in Oman, while linked in part to oil wealth, differs from the actual Gulf States because of the stagnation of the country under Sultan Said. Education was firmly restricted and until 1970, those Omanis who sought to better themselves escaped and educated their children abroad, which is why all educated Omani women, and men, were raised outside Oman.

It is still too soon for any native-born Omani to have graduated, and, particularly in Oman, there is the tremendous task of educating the illiterate tribes of the interior, who are still cut off by great mountain masses from the coastal towns.

The Omani girl who discussed the following subjects of equality, marriage and sex, wishes to remain anonymous as she is well-known in her country. Twenty-nine years old, she has been married for seven years, and is employed in the department of social welfare and is widely travelled.

'It depends what you mean by "women's liberation". If you mean having the same rights as men, we do. Sexual equality exists in every sense, except a domestic one. We have the same jobs for equal pay and we are also more liberated than other Gulf girls. The only women who wear *purdah* are the Dhofaris and the women of the Batinah Coast.

'Neither do we mind having our picture taken which, as you know, is virtually impossible in places like Qatar and the Emirates. But while we wear Western clothes, if it's not trousers, the dress is maxi, not by custom, but simply because we do not like men staring at our legs.

'Still in Oman there are timeless traditions surrounding social life and marriage. As in the Gulf, single girls live at home and although young people do not agree, parents still do not like them to meet the man before they marry him.

'Child marriages still occur in the interior. As a girl doesn't go to school, she has nothing to do and is something of a burden on the family. Then there is the dowry, a present from the husband to his bride, but many parents keep it for themselves. A poor family may also demand much more than he can afford, so if it is more than OR300 (about $500) he can get court permission to marry and a father cannot prevent it.

'Some of these children are only nine or ten when they marry, although the marriage is not consummated until they reach puberty. We, the educated townswomen, are not pressing for changes as it is a matter which has to be resolved by the family concerned. And so today it is quite true that all marriages in the interior, and some in Muscat, follow the traditional customs.

'Although I am broad-minded, even I had to marry in the traditional way as my parents wanted; to refuse would have meant being ostracised and probably no marriage at all. What happens is that the husband will consult the *mullah* to determine the most auspicious time to wed, according to the stars. The *mullah* will also tell him, even to the precise minute, when he should take his bride.

'After we married at the mosque, I returned home and awaited my husband who arrived amid much chatter, with his family. I wore a green dress, don't ask my why, it's custom, as you wear white in the West, and I lay waiting for him in an upstairs bedroom, especially prepared by my own family. Finally he came up and took me, quickly, without any foreplay since if one becomes too wet, this dilutes the blood, which must prove one is a virgin.

'This over, my elder sister came to help me, removing the white cloth from the nuptial bed and placing it on a silver tray which a servant carried out for my husband's parents to inspect. On seeing the fresh stains, everyone rejoiced and started eating and drinking and giving money to the poor. It's not a very nice moment for the bride though, don't you agree?'

'People are honest in Oman,' said Wahda Ahmed Masoud, the first woman police officer in the Sultanate and today director of the Royal Oman Women's Police Force. 'There is very little crime and I can't remember a case of rape.'

A diminutive 26, Wahda was born in Zanzibar, where her father had fled to escape the tyranny of Sultan Said.

'My mother died when I was three,' she said, as we spoke in her office overlooking the police cadet's parade-ground. 'My grandmother brought up my sister and me — my sister is also in the force, as a plainclothes CID woman.

'Because of the political trouble in Zanzibar, we moved to Uganda where I married an Omani at the age of 15. We had a daughter, but it ended in divorce,' she added shyly. 'In 1971, we returned with many others to our Omani homeland, where I commenced work in a bank. During this year I grew interested in working as a policewoman, so I left to become the first recruit in Oman.

'Because of the war in Dhofar, women were desparately needed as airport security officers, which is what I did, on completing my course. I was alone for six months, before other girls joined, but today, 32 women have graduated. We get equal pay for the same training as men in gymnastics, first aid, geography, criminal investigation and Arabic. We are also instructed in self-defence and judo.'

Wahda stands five foot nothing in her smart blue maxi-skirt, white shirt and navy piped cap. How would she manage judo in a skirt?

'I don't know,' she laughed. 'During the training we wear a divided skirt over trousers.'

'The entry age is fifteen years and if a girl is married, we must have her husband's consent. They live in a separate block to the men and are allowed home on Friday. Graduates start as security officers for Gulf Air and as warders at Jahali Prison.'

'Why don't Omani policewomen have a rank? This is an injustice when they are otherwise treated as equal to the policemen?' I enquired.

'I don't know,' Wahda replied, and I realised why the big Amin-type police officer had been so angry when I had asked to see the 'Women's Chief of Police'.

'There isn't one!' he'd bellowed.

In 1972, at the age of 24, Naashiah Soud al-Kharusi became the first electrical and communications engineer, man or woman, in the Sultanate of Oman; today she is the senior engineer with seven men working under her and her job involves every aspect of telephone communications in the country. Naashiah, too, was born in Zanzibar where her family had moved from Oman. Her mother married at fourteen and unlike many Omanis and Gulf Arabs, her father did not take a second wife.

'I went to school in Zanzibar until I was ten. My parents then sent me to boarding school in Cairo from where I attended university, taking my degree in electrical engineering and communications.'

'While still a student, I married a Jordanian, the father of my seven-year-old son, but we divorced, and I took Mulham to Aden, where we moved after the *coup d'état* in Zanzibar.'

'When we returned to Oman in 1971, at first I could not find a job and because I thought the government would never employ a woman, I did not bother to apply for one,' she said.

'However, even in 1972, there was no one responsible for telecommunications, so I was offered the job, a tremendous strain, since

Naashiah Soud al-Kharusi, the first tele-communications engineer in Oman.

نعشية سعود الخاروسي . أول مهندسة في كهربائية الإتصالات التليفونية في عمان .

I was responsible for a project worth nine million rials.

'I have married again, but I don't see my husband much as he is Consular Attaché in Kuwait. I would join him were it not for my job, as it is not good living apart like this. But I am still not finished,' she added, 'I want to make my master's degree, probably in computer science.'

'But you must have difficulties in such a masculine environment,' I said, quite amazed.

'Ah, but I am not the same as you see me now. In the office I am very serious, I wear trousers and don't bother about make-up. Sometimes at night, when I meet one of the men, he does not recognise me, and his wife does not believe I am his boss,' she smiled. 'They appreciate me,' she continued modestly, 'maybe for my experience, since I work hard and always try to learn from others. Only once have I experienced discrimination, when I was advised to refuse an invitation to attend a function for heads of telecommunications in Abu Dhabi.'

'There, of course, no women work as yet and I would have been the only one present, a breach of etiquette in traditional Bedouin society.'

One hopes this remarkable woman may be typical of the next generation of women in the Gulf. Beautiful, intelligent, liberated and adhering only to Islamic code of neither smoking nor drinking, Naashiah has never worn *purdah,* and drives to work.

Running Oman's vital communications system, proves what a contribution she and other women can make to their own country, and the Gulf as a whole. Whether she realises it or not, the liberation of women in the interior rests on her shoulders.

Appendix

BAHRAIN

Entry Requirements: All visitors except British passport-holders require a visa. Smallpox inoculation, cholera and TAB advised with anti-malaria precautions.

Tipping: 100 fils per case.

Accommodation:
  Gulf Hotel: Post Box 580, Manama, Bahrain.
  Hilton Hotel: Post Box 1090, Manama, Bahrain.
  Delmon Hotel: Post Box 26, Manama, Bahrain.
  Moon Plaza: Post Box 247, Manama, Bahrain.
  Sahara Hotel: Post Box 839, Manama, Bahrain.
  Middle East: Post Box 838, Manama, Bahrain.
  Tylos Hotel: Post Box 1086, Manama, Bahrain.

Business Hours:
  Offices: 08.00–13.00. 15.00–17.00.
  Shops: 08.00–11.00 and 12.30. 16.00–19.00.
  Banks: 08.00–11.30.

Electric Current: 230 volts AC, 50 cycles.

Further Information:
  Embassy of the State of Bahrain,
  98 Gloucester Road,
  London SW7 4AU.

  Ministry of Information,
  Post Box 2053,
  Manama,
  Bahrain.

KUWAIT

Entry Requirements: A visa is required for which a local sponsor is necessary. Smallpox inoculation with cholera and yellow fever if coming from an infected area. TAB advised.

Tipping: 100 fils per case.

Accommodation:
 Kuwait Hilton: Post Box 5996, Kuwait.
 Kuwait Sheraton: Post Box 5902, Kuwait.
 Golden Beach: Post Box 3483, Kuwait.
 Bristol: Post Box 3531, Kuwait.
 Sahara: Post Box 2461, Kuwait.
 Universal: Post Box 5593, Kuwait.
 Messilah Hotel: Post Box 3522, Safat, Kuwait.

Business Hours:
 Offices: 09.00–13.00. 15.30–19.30.
 Shops: 09.00–13.00. 15.30–19.30.
 Banks: 08.30–12.00.

Electric Current: 220 volts AC.

Further Information:
 Embassy of Kuwait,
 40 Devonshire Street,
 London W1.

 Ministry of Information,
 Mubarak al-Kabir Street,
 Kuwait.

QATAR

Entry Requirements: All visitors, except British passport-holders, require a visa. Smallpox and cholera inoculation.

Tipping: QR100 per case.

Accommodation:
 Gulf Hotel: Post Box 1911, Doha, Qatar.
 Oasis Hotel: Post Box 717, Doha, Qatar.
 New Doha Palace: Post Box 710, Doha, Qatar.

Business Hours:
 Offices: 08.00–12.30. 15.00–18.00.
 Shops: 09.00–12.30. 15.00–18.00

Banks: 7.30–11.30.

Electric Current: 220/240 volts AC, 50 cycles.

Further Information:
  Embassy of Qatar,
  9 Reeves Mews,
  London W1.

  Ministry of Information,
  Post Box 1836,
  Doha,
  Qatar.

UNITED ARAB EMIRATES

Entry Requirements: All visitors must possess a visa. A local sponsor is necessary to obtain a visa. Smallpox inoculation with cholera and yellow fever if arriving from infected area. TAB immunisation recommended.

Tipping: DH1 per case.

Accommodation:
  Abu Dhabi:
  Abu Dhabi Hilton: Post Box 877, Abu Dhabi.
  Khalidia Palace: Post Box 4040, Abu Dhabi.
  Al-Ain Palace: Post Box 33, Abu Dhabi.
  Al-Ain Hilton: Al-Ain, Abu Dhabi.

  Dubai:
  Dubai Inter-Continental: Post Box 476, Dubai.
  Carlton Towers Hotel: Post Box 1955, Dubai.
  Ambassador Hotel: Post Box 3226, Dubai.
  Phoenicia Hotel: Post Box 4467, Dubai.
  Bustan Hotel: Post Box 1533, Dubai.

  Sharjah:
  Carlton Sharjah: Post Box 1198, Sharjah.
  Sheba Hotel: Post Box 486, Sharjah.
  Summerland Motel: Post Box 1081, Sharjah.

  Ras al-Khaimah
  Ras al Khaimah Hotel: Post Box 56, R.A.K.

Electric Current: 220/240 volts AC.

Business Hours:
   Offices: 07.00–12.00. 16.00–19.00
   Shops: 09.00–13.00. 16.00–19.00.
   Banks: 08.00–12.00.

Further Information:
   Embassy of the United Arab Emirates,
   30 Princes Gate,
   London SW7.

   Ministry of Information and Culture,
   Post Box 17,
   Abu Dhabi,
   United Arab Emirates.

SULTANATE OF OMAN

Entry Requirements: A visa will be issued against a letter from the local contact company, stating purpose of visit and dates. This should be supported by a letter from the Arab Chamber of Commerce. A 'No Objections Certificate' is required by business men born outside the UK. Smallpox, cholera, yellow fever inoculations required. TAB inoculation and anti-malarial precautions if visiting Dhofar.

Tipping: Optional.

Accommodation:
   Gulf Hotel: Post Box 4455, Muscat.
   Al-Falaj Hotel: Post Box 456, Muscat.
   Muscat Inter-Continental: Muscat.

Business Hours:
   Offices: 08.30–14.00.
   Shops: 08.00–13.00. 16.00–18.30.
   Banks: 08.00–12.00.

Electric Current: 220/240V AC, 50 cycles.

Further Information:
   Embassy of the Sultanate of Oman,
   64 Ennismore Gardens,
   London SW7.

   Ministry of Information and Culture,
   Post Box 600,
   Ruwi, Oman.

Bibliography

Personal Column, Sir Charles Belgrave.
Welcome to Bahrain, James Belgrave.
Looking for Dilumn, Geoffrey Bibby.
Bahrain Trade Directory.
Antiquities of Bahrain, Bahrain Archeological and Historical Society.
Arabia Without Sultans, Fred Halliday.
The Emirates, UAE Embassy Magazine.
Arabian Sands, Wilfred Thesiger.
Farewell to Arabia, David Holden.
Oman – A History, Wendell Phillips.
Unknown Oman, Wendell Phillips.
Muscat and Oman, Ian Skeet.
The Koran.
Role of the Public Works Department, UAE government.
Arab States of the Lower Gulf – People, Politics and Petroleum, John Duke Anthony.
The United Arab Emirates, Michael Tomkinson.
Arab Countries, Travintal Ltd.
The United Arab Emirates – An Economic and Social Survey, Kevin G. Fenelon.
The Businessman's Guide to Bahrain, Qatar, the UAE and Sultanate of Oman, Standard Chartered Bank Group.
Hints to Businessmen, UAE and Sultanate of Oman, British Overseas Board of Trade.
Notes on Qatar, Abu Dhabi and Bahrain, Hong Kong Bank Group.
Middle East Annual Review.
Businessman's Guide to the Arabian Gulf States, Said Salah.
Falconry as a Sport, Zaid bin Sultan al-Nahayan.
International Conference on Falconry and Conservation, 10-18 December 1976, Abu Dhabi.
The Gulf States and Sultanate of Oman, British Airways.

Also the special reports from *The Times, Financial Times, Guardian* and *Gulf Mirror.*

Middle East Economic Development, Kuwaiti Digest, The Emirates News, Kuwaiti Times, The Middle East Magazine, notes from Dubai Museum *Magazine,* Doha Museum, and official publications by the Ministries of Information.

About the Author

Born in Sydney, Australia, Christine Osborne is a free-lance journalist and photographer who has contributed to worldwide newspapers and magazines on travel, sociology and related customs.

In 1970-1 she received the Pacific Area Travel Writers' award for travel journalism.

This is her first book, a result of frequent visits to the Arabian Gulf between 1974 and 1976.

Index

Abu Dhabi Women's Association 194
Adair, Red 89
advertising 23
aid, economic 46-7, 116, 119, 120, 122, 124, 175, 190
alcohol, consumption of 65, 104, 164
al-Garhoud Bridge, the 97
antiques 183-4
astrology, importance of, in dating weddings 197
Australia, trade commission of, 23

banking 24-5, 36, 68, 110, 116
Bedouin 33, 34, 39, 41, 43, 50, 59, 63, 74, 75, 87, 88, 112, 124, 128, 130, 135, 141, 144, 146, 180, 181, 187, 200
boat-building 28, 29, 31-2, 34, 45, 115, 117, 132
bride price 75, 78, 167

camel, the 166-171
careers (for women) 189, 190
cautery 141
childbirth 105
Children and Mothers' Welfare Society 190
costume 178-183

'Damavand Line' 148
development, economic 96-9, 101, 107-11, 133, 135, 136-9, 153-5
Dhofar, civil war in 147-9, 198
discrimination, sexual 187, 200
divorce 191, 195
dowry 189, 191, 196

expatriot workers 25, 28, 34, 40, 52, 54, 67, 69, 75, 78, 101, 102, 104, 113, 141, 166, 185; homosexuality among 75
Eurobonds 41

Faisal, King 41
falconry 171-5, 177-8
farming 46, 56-7, 58, 75, 82-6, 106, 110, 112, 119, 120, 121, 122, 123-4, 142, 143, 144, 147, 153
federation 61, 63, 87
fishing 28, 29, 39, 46, 57-8, 89, 108, 115, 117, 119, 123, 127-8, 140, 144, 147, 151, 153-4

gambling 120, 121

Hamed bin Mohammed al-Qasimi, Sheikh 20, 127
'Hornbeam Line' 148
housing 25-8, 43, 73-4, 111, 116, 129, 165; corruption in seeking contracts for 72-3; cost of 137; prefabricated 23, 73; shortage of 26, 102
Hussain, Fatima Sheikha 73, 82, 186, 193-5

immigration, illegal 78-9
incense trade 146, 154
inflation 101, 136, 171, 183
investment 41-2, 51-4, 79-80, 102, 107, 111, 123
irrigation 30, 57, 58, 82, 84-5, 102, 143
Isa bin Sulman al-Khalifa, Sheikh 17, 18, 20, 25, 26, 30, 50, 180, 191

Khalid, King 81
Khalifa bin Hamad al-Thani, Sheikh 48, 49, 53, 54, 55
Koran, the 56, 120, 142, 158, 164, 181, 185, 186, 191, 195
Kuwait Fund for Arab Economic Development 46-7

land reclamation 67, 97
Lebanon, civil war in 24
living, cost of 136; standard of 44

Manama 28-9
marriage 189, 190-1, 192, 194, 196; of children 196, 197
milk, consumption of 153
money changers 141
Musandam Peninsula 130, 136

oil 28, 29, 31, 33, 34-5, 36, 43, 44, 45, 46, 48-9, 50, 53, 57, 59, 61, 63-6, 88-9, 102, 104, 105, 106, 115, 117, 119, 120, 124, 129, 133, 135-6, 142, 148, 186, 192
'Operation Halwa' 149
Organisation of Arab Petroleum Exporting Countries

Saqr bin Muhammed al-Qasimi,
  Sheikh 105, 106, 109, 110,
  111-2, 113, 121, 125
Shakhbut, Sheikh 65-6, 68, 133, 162
slavery 81, 117, 128, 133, 154-5,
  181, 184
smuggling 92, 94, 96
Sulman, Sheikh 20

telecommunications 24, 25, 55-6,
  101, 121, 122, 139, 142, 155,
  198, 200
tourism 81-2, 101, 106, 112-3,
  115, 129, 155
trade 90, 92, 94, 108, 127, 132,
  189; past 19, 34, 38, 49, 67,
  146-7
'Treaty of Peace in Perpetuity' 121

virginity, proof of immediate loss
  of, on marriage 197

weaving 29-30
welfare 43-4, 48, 104-5, 141,
  151, 160, 187, 189
Wildlife Management Board (Sind)
  175
Women's Year (1975) 190

Zayed bin Sultan al-Hahyan,
  Sheikh 61, 63, 65, 66, 68, 73,
  81, 82, 84, 85, 86, 87-8,
  160, 161, 171, 175, 193, 194,
  195

(OAPEC) 22, 98
Organisation of Petroleum
  Exporting Countries (OPEC)
  35, 56, 135, 171

past, lack of appreciation for 50
pearling 17, 18, 18-21, 29, 31, 32,
  34, 38, 39, 45, 89, 117, 162,
  192
'Perpetual Maritime Treaty', the
  (1853) 61
pottery 29, 45, 81, 124, 132, 166-7
prohibition 40
prostitution 104

Qabos bin Said, Sultan 130,
  133, 134, 138, 141, 142, 147,
  154, 155, 196, 197

Ramadan 28, 52, 158
Rashid Hassan al-Khalifa, Sheikh 25
Rashid bin Humaid al-Nuaimi,
  Sheikh 116, 154
bin Rashid al-Moalla, Sheikh 120
Rashid bin Saeed al-Maktoum,
  Sheikh 88, 90, 96, 97, 98, 99,
  102, 104, 108, 111, 171, 175
re-afforestation 84, 165
Royal Oman Women's Police
  Force 197-8

Sabah al-Salam al-Sabah, Sheikh
  34, 41, 47
Said, Sultan 65